WHAT PEOPLE AF
DANIEL DOS SAN'

"*Soccer in Your Back* very fun way, presents activity. This innovative approach of bringing soccer home will produce immediate results for parents and children; it will enhance the Soccer Clubs' programs and bring a new dimension to soccer in the U.S."

>Joe McGuigan,
>Head Coach, Men's Soccer
>Sacred Heart University
>Fairfield, CT

"A must have for soccer parents! *Soccer in Your Backyard* returns us to the grass roots of the game by making soccer an enjoyable experience for both child and parent. Dos Santos has made both the mental and psychological aspects of the game easy to learn."

>Ricky Zambrano
>Head Coach Men's Soccer
>St. Thomas University
>Miami, FL

"Through games and exercises, *Soccer in Your Backyard,* imparts an approach to the sport that is both simple and fun. Parents and children alike should find it useful in teaching as well as learning basic soccer skills."

>Rocco Paul Valluzzo
>Sports Editor, Weston Forum
>Weston, CT

"*Soccer in Your Backyard* shows that parents, children and coaches can work together as a team. The concept that '*it takes a village to raise a child*' truly comes out in this book, and all of us have the power and responsibility to be that village."

>Fran Ault, L.C.S.W
>School Counselor
>Miami, FL

"Daniel dos Santos has a very unique technique in uniting the family, parents and children with a soccer ball, providing a totally entertaining experience while learning soccer skills."

Nadine Oundjian, parent
Weston, CT

"The dos Santos's philosophy brings out the best we can experience through learning. What better way to bring parents and children together than through the life experiences and values the sport of soccer can teach when taught properly in a positive environment."

C. Donald Cook
Director of Athletics
Sacred Heart University
Fairfield, CT

"During my seven years as a Soccer Commissioner and coach, I have reviewed many books on training youth that only focus on the technical and tactical aspects of the game. Daniel dos Santos's innovative philosophy of involving the family is a key factor, the energy boost youth soccer needs in the United States to ensure that our youth will continue with the game."

Pedro Correa
P.S.N.A.A. Soccer Commissioner
Miami, FL

"Teaching soccer skills is only part of what Daniel does. He also teaches the child discipline, confidence, competition and sportsmanship. The greatest thing is that he is not only teaching the sport but is educating the child."

Emilio Sotil, parent
Weston CT

"As an instructor, player and advocate of soccer, Daniel dos Santos has few peers. His book, *Soccer in Your Backyard*, serves many worthwhile purposes, including strengthening family ties."

Don Harrison
Manager, News Bureau
Sacred Heart University
Fairfield, CT

Soccer in Your Backyard

An Innovative Approach
to Improving Your Child's Soccer
Skills While Enhancing Your
Family's Quality Time

Daniel dos Santos

Reneda
Publishing House

Miami, FL
U.S.A.

Published by:
Reneda Publishing House
P.O. Box 170710
Hialeah, FL 33017 - 0710

Copyright © 1997 by Daniel dos Santos

All rights reserved. No part of this book may be reproduced or transmitted in any form or by any means, electronic or mechanical, including photocopying, without permission in writing from the publisher, except in the case of a brief quotation within critical articles or reviews.

Edited by Linda S. Zuker
Cover photo by Rocco Paul Valluzzo
Drawings by George Briz
Cover design by Action Graphic, Miami, FL

Photo credits:

Rocco Paul Valluzzo, pages: 31,35,52,54,55,56,58,61,64,66, 68,74,75(bottom),80,81(bottom),82,83,84,86,92(top),93,94, 95,101,102,106,109(top),111,112,113,116(top),118,119,120, 122,124,125,128,129,130,131 and 132.

Deborah O'Brien, pages: 25,26,27,28,39,45,48,49,70,71, 92(bottom) and 134.

George Briz, pages: 51,75(top),78,98, and 99.

Sancho Photography, Author's photo, page 7.

Library of Congress Catalog Card Number 98-71409

ISBN 0-9664114-0-4

Printed in the United States of America by:
Hallmark Press, Inc., North Miami, FL

Disclaimer: Participants of any sport must be in good health and physical condition. The exercises presented in this book (especially the bicycle kick) require adult supervision.

TABLE OF CONTENTS

About the Author		07
Foreword		09
Introduction		11
1.	**My Soccer Philosophy**	15
2.	**Dribbling**	23
3.	**Passing**	43
4.	**Kicking**	60
5.	**Ball Control**	79
6.	**Juggling**	91
7.	**Heading**	100
8.	**The Old Mattress**	107
9.	**Reaction, Agility and Strength**	123
10.	**Parent-Coach Relationship**	135
11.	**Programs To Be Considered**	140
12.	**If You Get Involved...**	145
Conclusion		150
Glossary of Common Soccer Terms		152

ACKNOWLEDGEMENTS

This book wouldn't be possible without the encouragement, support and extraordinary patience of my family: Marilyn, Michael and Christina. Thank you, guys.

Special thanks to Linda S. Zuker for her editing contribution to the book.

A million thanks to Michael Gates who patiently listened to my thoughts and helped me organize this work.

Thanks to Rose Cabrera for the first proofreading of this book.

My gratitude to George and Antonella Briz for their unconditional support and willingness to help me in all my endeavors.

My immense appreciation to Teresa Fernandez, a school counselor and friend, who spent lots of hours giving me her insights on the book's final stage.

I would like to acknowledge the following friends and family for their participation in the photo sessions of this book in which they endured countless hours under the sun with endless enthusiasm:

> Rocco, Andrea and Allison Valluzzo; Deborah O'Brien; Fernando Fernandes; Steve and Peter Scher; Helen, Max and Zach During; Peter Oundjian and his son Peter; Kade and Leslie Krichko; Jessica and Betsey Gilbertie; Kyle Sherwood, Rosemarie Dixon, Hames Maria D'Costa and Andre Williams; George, Antonella, Emmanuel, Maria Isabel and Marc Briz.

Finally, thanks to all the parents and children who have participated in my soccer camps, after-school programs and international events through the years.

About the Author

Daniel dos Santos is from Uruguay, South America. From playing first division soccer in Artigas, he moved to Montevideo to join the legendary soccer club, Peñarol's youth teams. He played professional soccer for seven years on teams such as Danubio and Villa Española of Uruguay. At the international level, he played nine games for his country.

The founder and director of the All-American soccer school, Daniel is also the founder and president of Global Youth, Inc., an organization committed to educating children through sports. For the past eight years in Connecticut, he has been the skills director for the Westport Soccer Association, the Weston Soccer Club and Landmark Academy. In addition, he has conducted soccer camps and clinics in the U.S., Thailand, Japan, India and Uruguay as well as international programs with Brazil and Guatemala.

Daniel holds an M.B.A. from Sacred Heart University in Fairfield, Connecticut. He was awarded the medal of Academic Excellence for the class of 1990 as well as the Student-Athlete award for the class of 1990. The same year, he was selected All-American, playing for Sacred Heart University. He was the president of Phi Sigma Iota, Delta Kappa 132 Chapter, International Honor Society from 1990 to 1992.

His ability to speak Spanish, Portuguese, English and Italian and his passion for children and soccer has made him a tireless traveler to anywhere in the world where his help is needed.

He is an avid reader. His hobbies are traveling and camping, which he enjoys sharing with his wife Marilyn and their children Michael and Christina.

To the love of my life, Marilyn

FOREWORD

On my office wall, right above my desk, hangs a photo of a goalkeeper diving and catching an extremely difficult ball. The caption reads: "EXCELLENCE: SOME SUCCEED BECAUSE THEY ARE DESTINED TO; MOST SUCCEED BECAUSE THEY ARE **DETERMINED** TO." I have always believed in these words which have become my motto. Everything I have accomplished in life has been largely through determination.

As a child, my first school years were overshadowed by extreme shyness. Even though I was always an outstanding student, I would not raise my hand in class or volunteer for any group activity. Due to the concern and recommendation of my second grade teacher, my parents decided to enroll me in an organized soccer program. That was the best decision they ever made. Within a year and a half of playing organized soccer, not only did my skills improve tremendously; but, more importantly, I changed from a shy, young boy to an outspoken, confident one. My soccer skills improved in a matter of two or three seasons. Thus, I gained self-confidence, motivation and leadership skills.

In the fourth grade, I was a totally different child. By then, I had developed an eagerness for improving myself and for learning not only in school but also in sports. I would wait for my teachers and coaches after class and practice to ask them about the next lesson. As soon as I learned something new, I wanted to know what I would learn next.

10 *Soccer in Your Backyard*

As a direct result of those positive changes I had achieved through soccer, my parents became involved and committed to a sport which was already a part of our family.

That determination which began with soccer always made me work harder than my peers. In order to improve, I learned early in life to compete against myself. For example, until I was eight-years-old, only one boy in the neighborhood owned a soccer ball. We were poor, and a ball was not in my parents' budget. Yet that didn't stop me. My desire to improve made me learn to juggle with flowers (jasmine), then with oranges and even with balls made out of old socks which my grandmother would sew together for me. I had an opportunity to practice with a real ball only when I went to train with my team or when the boy who owned the only ball was in a sufficiently good mood to let me borrow it.

That desire to quench my thirst for knowledge continues to predominate my life. To improve myself has been my drive; to be better than yesterday, my own requirement; to give my one-hundred percent, my obligation; to do the unexpected, my challenge; to teach, my passion, and to communicate my inner self to others, my dream.

INTRODUCTION

Welcome to **Soccer in Your Backyard!** Thank you for being interested in soccer. Everyday thousands of families around the nation are joining the soccer phenomenon.

Soccer has become very popular, because parents are realizing that it is the best game through which to introduce children to sports. Every child, regardless of his physical characteristics or ability, can play soccer and have fun.

As a sport, soccer offers a wealth of possibilities through which parents and coaches can work together. Soccer helps the child improve his skills and body coordination as well as any special need he may have, such as low self-esteem or lack of confidence, drive, leadership or social skills.

It is in this spirit of learning through sports that **Soccer in Your Backyard** presents the necessary skills to play soccer, "camouflaged" as fun games. Hopefully, it will help parents make the time spent with their children at home more enjoyable. Moreover, my hope is to make soccer a family activity, challenging both the children's and the parents' creativity and imagination. Its objective is to improve the family's quality time when parents and children happen to be united through a soccer ball.

Throughout the years that I have been teaching in the United States, South America and Asia, I have witnessed a world of difference that parental involvement makes in a child's overall development.

12   *Soccer in Your Backyard*

The key elements for the success of your child are MOTIVATION and PERSISTENCE. You know your child's personality better than anyone else. Based on that fact and on my experience working with children, I suggest using soccer and soccer-related games as vehicles to continue discovering your child's strengths and weaknesses. I am a strong believer that if we can achieve a high level of motivation through soccer, we can work miracles for your child in a short period of time. This book can also help you find fun games to play with your child after work or on weekends. The activities are also highly effective when used at parties or whenever your child's friends get together.

You can be your child's best

M O T I V A T O R.

Why should one play soccer in the backyard?

Experience has shown me that the backyard is the best place to develop soccer skills, especially for children between the ages of five and twelve.

I trained in my backyard until I was 17-years-old, even though I was already playing first-division soccer at the age of 15. Still today my backyard is the most comfortable place for me to enhance my skills and maintain good physical fitness.

I think of the backyard as a laboratory where you can experiment with different formulas or even invent new ones. If you cause an "explosion" there, no one will ever know about it. Therefore, it will not cause embarrassment for anyone. This is also an ideal, safe place for children to build their confidence and overcome their fear of making mistakes, as this is a concern in any learning process.

As I do in my teaching, "camouflage" the skills behind exercises or games to make it fun for the children. Try to understand and help teach the skills and techniques as best you can, all the while maintaining a fun and comfortable atmosphere.

To facilitate both my writing and your reading of the book, I have used the third-person pronoun, "he," to represent both boys and girls in general.

I hope you will enjoy these games with your family, relatives and friends. More importantly, I want you to understand that you are the best engine to propel the skills, confidence, and motivation your child will need to succeed in our competitive world. Moreover, through the game of soccer, you can penetrate the barriers of communication that children and parents often build.

My definition of "backyard soccer" is broad and includes soccer in the park, pick-up games, family soccer and "street" soccer. It is my belief that this concept of soccer is what the U.S. youth soccer movement needs in order to effectively link parents and children. Backyard soccer will produce parents with practical soccer skills and knowledge of the game. This will enable them to provide the necessary "back stage" strength to "fuel" their children's long-lasting participation in soccer.

Hopefully, through anecdotes and my philosophy, I can offer you another key to open your imagination to further enhance your child's overall development.

14   *Soccer in Your Backyard*

This book also intends to encourage parents, if possible, to play soccer. It is important that you practice at home with your family and also that you go to the field, get together with other adults to organize an informal parents' game once in a while. If you are physically able, parents' games are fun; besides, you exercise and socialize at the same time.

By learning more about soccer, making soccer a family activity, challenging your child to improve his skills at home and playing adult soccer, you will be setting an example. If followed by other parents throughout the country, this will become the missing piece of the puzzle that will establish soccer as a solid sport in the American culture.

Daniel dos Santos
Miami, April 1999

1

MY SOCCER PHILOSOPHY

Soccer is a game which combines the creativity and skills of individuals with a supportive team structure. I coach by presenting the facts to the players (the hows and whys of the game) while encouraging players' input, creativity and inspiration.

I never impose my ideas on the players, because that creates fear to do only what the coach wants. Instead, I present the best strategies and let the players figure things out on their own. By doing this, I encourage the thinking process and the development of their own personal styles. Once I teach them the basics, I allow them to follow their instincts to explore their given talents within a framework of mutual trust and respect.

In this chapter, I will first describe the different stages of my coaching methodology. Of course, each child responds differently, but this will give you an overall idea of my teaching approach. Then, I will specifically detail the qualities that need to be taught to players under the heading of sportsmanship. Finally, I will give you an idea of what qualities I seek in my assistant coaches.

TEACHING METHODOLOGY

CREATE A FRIENDLY AND TRUSTFUL ATMOSPHERE.

First, I break the ice with jokes, personal stories and games. We connect. When the children feel comfortable, I evaluate children's skill levels and prospective field positions. To accomplish this, I create two teams, throw out a ball and allow the children to play freely. From this UNSTRUCTURED game environment, I observe the children's skills and the field positions they spontaneously choose to play.

If you ever need to run a tryout, try the abovementioned method. The word "tryout" may cause anxiety in some children; but by giving them what appears to be free time with the ball, you encourage them to play without fears or pressures.

CAMOUFLAGE SOCCER SKILLS AS FUN GAMES.

I incorporate the soccer skills I want to teach with FUN games such as Sharks, UFO Invasion, King of the Mountain, Rambo, Superman, etc. Children have fun, and they feel like participating. These games allow me to complete my assessment process.

PREPARE THE GROUND TO PLANT THE SEEDS.

I perform a skill demonstration, such as a difficult move or kick. I do this to obtain respect from the group. At the same time, I tell them a short story about my professional days.

WATER THE SEEDS WITH MOTIVATION.

At this point, I go into specific skill training. The children are now ready to mentally absorb and learn from me. I build confidence and assurance. I say: "You can do it. You will make it, if you believe in yourself. You have the potential." Then I try to relate to the children at their level. I tell them how difficult it was for me to do what they are trying to accomplish at their age. I also promise them a reward, such as a trophy or a medal, if they achieve a certain level of skill. Thus, they have something concrete to which they can look forward in the short run, if they put forth a certain amount of effort and achieve goals.

An extremely important element is to teach them to compete against themselves. They should beat their own records!

NOURISH THE SEEDS.

I follow the development of the child's soccer skills, his behavior within a group, his self-esteem and his leadership potential. I encourage and reassure them: "Be yourself. Don't follow the others. Don't change your own personality." I give them the green light to make mistakes: "Don't be afraid of making mistakes, because we learn from our mistakes." Communication with parents increases substantially.

This is a period of intense training and working on overcoming personality weaknesses. Children are reevaluated, and I assign field positions to the players. My team system and game strategy are always designed according to the types of players I have. Usually, a team has two or three outstanding players, while the rest are good, average or below average. From that mix of abilities, I try to come up with a balanced team which will have a strong defense, a good play-maker in the midfield and someone in the forward line with the ability to score goals.

GIVE THEM FREEDOM.

The most important aspect of my coaching approach is that after I have explained the different functions of the three lines (defense-midfield-forward), and I am certain my players have clearly understood the concepts of covering for each other, **I allow them to move freely on the field.**

For example, a defender on my team knows that his job is to help protect our goal. However, if at any given moment of inspiration or creativity, he wants to start dribbling up the field to try to score a goal, he knows he can do that as long as a teammate covers for him. If he loses the ball near the other team's goal, he will have time to recover and retain peace of mind for two reasons: first, he knows he has the coach's green light to take a risk, and second, his field position is being covered by someone else.

THE BLOOMING STAGE.

We have arrived at the end of the cycle. Children experience great improvements in their skills and personalities. They make clearer decisions and are more motivated. They understand their roles on the team and feel more confident playing the game.

My Soccer Philosophy   19

SPORTSMANSHIP

Through the game of soccer, I teach my players not only to understand the game and their field positions, but equally important, to build their own personalities and playing styles. They should be the best **sportsmen** possible by becoming the following:

Committed. Players must always give one-hundred percent of themselves. If so, they will have the peace of mind that they did their best, regardless of the outcome of the game.

Responsible. Players take responsibility for their actions on and off the field. The team depends on them.

Respectful. Players must respect themselves, their coaches, teammates, opponents, referees and spectators.

Problem-solvers / Decision makers. Players learn to read the game, identify the other team's strengths and weaknesses and implement strategies.

Team players. Players must always consider the team before making any decision. The team comes first. They must provide others with opportunities and make sacrifices for the team.

Humble. Players are taught to never boast or brag about their abilities. They must never diminish or humiliate their own team members or rivals.

Confident. Players learn to be confident about what they can do on the field. They trust their skills. They have the full support of the coaches when making mistakes.

Risk-takers. At appropriate times in the game, it is important for players to take chances in order to succeed.

Individualistic. There are times when players must act alone. I give them guidelines on how to judge when this is necessary.

Creative / Spontaneous. Players are encouraged to do the unexpected, to follow their instincts, to do the unteachable.

Soccer is merely one way to teach children the value of these qualities. As they are necessary for success on the field and later in life, parents should reinforce these ideals and encourage their children to implement them at home and in school.

MY CODE FOR COACHES

Just as I instill in my players the above-mentioned values, I expect my assistant coaches to embody the following qualities. I find these may be helpful to parents, coaches, and soccer board members when assessing a coach's performance.

AS A COACH, YOU SHOULD:

LIKE CHILDREN.
If you don't, read no further.

LEAD BY EXAMPLE.
Children will imitate you.

BE A MOTIVATOR.
Children will like you.

HAVE FUN AND ENJOY YOURSELF.
Children will enjoy your teaching.

BE RESPECTFUL.
Children will respect you.

HAVE A GOOD SENSE OF HUMOR.
You will make hard work seem easy.

EMPATHIZE WITH THE CHILDREN.
Be realistic about children's limitations.

BE CREATIVE AND IMPROVISE.
Things do not always go as planned.

BE PATIENT.
If you are not, teaching is not for you.

AS A COACH, YOU SHOULD NOT:

BOSS OR BORE THE CHILDREN.
Children love to have fun.

MAKE CHILDREN WAIT IN LONG LINES OR GIVE LONG SPEECHES.
Children have short attention spans.

LOSE YOUR TEMPER OR YELL.
Children take things literally and can be easily hurt.

It is my hope that by now I have been able to convey to you my teaching philosophy and that you have a good understanding of my approach to coaching. The skills described in the following chapters are necessary for your child to play soccer. However, even if you know them already, always look beyond the games and exercises to see how they can be better adapted to suit your child's own needs and special characteristics. Moreover, this book encourages you to see soccer as another alternative in helping your child improve his overall personal development. How does your child react to challenges? How does he cope with frustrations? Does he get easily distracted or bored? Does he follow instructions? All these and more may be found through the sport he loves. May this backyard journey bring your family together by providing better soccer skills and an opportunity to play and laugh, to learn and grow and to strengthen communication and understanding.

2

DRIBBLING

What is dribbling?

Dribbling is the ability to maneuver the ball with all the surfaces of our feet to maintain possession and control of the ball. Dribbling makes soccer a colorful game. In a moment of inspiration, a lone player can masterfully dribble and fake his way through the entire opposing defense to score a goal.

How do we dribble?

As we jog or run, we move the ball using any part of the foot. We should pat the ball with soft kicks, just hard enough for the ball to stay a few inches away from the foot (ideally not more than two feet).

Why do we need to dribble?

1) To create our own opportunity to score.
2) To maintain possession of the ball until we can pass the ball to a teammate.
3) To move the ball to a different part of the field to create opportunities for the team.

Like a basketball player uses his hands to move the ball around his waist or under his legs, a soccer player does all that and more with his feet.

Therefore, the first thing we need to do is to teach our children to develop feet coordination. I call the work that we do with our feet: **footwork.**

In order to motivate children under the age of eight to practice footwork, I tell them they need to learn to drive the ball as mom or dad drives a car. I accomplish this with the following exercise.

Each child stands behind the ball. Then we pretend to turn on the car engines. We make the appropriate sound, "VROOM...VROOM", and we begin driving our cars (dribbling). We drive forward a bit, and I yell "BRAKES!" Everybody makes screeching sounds, and we STOP the car by placing the sole of the foot on top of the ball. From that position, we REVERSE and drive backwards by continuously rolling the ball backwards with the sole of the foot, while hopping on the other foot.

Dribbling 25

There are two ways to drive our car (move the ball) sideways: with the sole or the outside of the foot. Both of these approaches can be used to move the ball right or left. I will describe how to drive the ball to the left. Simply reverse all directions in order to go right.

1) Stand to the left of the ball. Place the sole of your right foot on top of the ball. With the right foot roll the ball to the left. As this foot touches the ground, walk to the left using your left foot. Therefore, you should roll the ball and then walk; roll the ball and then walk. With some practice, you can increase the pace to roll and then run.

2) Stand completely to the right side of the ball and, with the outside of your left foot, repeatedly pat the ball lightly while moving to the left side. Increase the pace when you are able.

NOTE: When dribbling the ball, always hit the ball gently to keep it as close to your feet as possible (two feet maximum).

MORE EXERCISES

Begin by positioning your best foot on top of the ball. Open your arms a little bit for balance. With the sole of the foot, start moving the ball a few inches to the right and to the left. Then move the ball forward and backwards from the same position. All your body weight is on the stationary foot. You can also move while doing this exercise. To do so, you have to hop. The foot which is controlling the ball always stays on top of it, never touching the ground. To move, rely only on the other foot. Progressively increase the pace. Ideally, although it is more difficult, attempt to do the same exercise with the weaker foot.

IN BETWEEN THE FEET

Position the ball in between your feet and spread your legs shoulder wide. With the inside of one foot, pass the ball to the other foot. Keep on passing the ball back and forth from one foot to the other. As you do this, jump up a bit. Get a rhythm; it should be like dancing.

PUSH AND PULL

This is a fast movement in which you push the ball forward and pull it back immediately. Your right foot is on the ground behind the ball. With the inside surface of the right foot, push the ball forward to the fullest leg extension. When the initial motion ends, place the sole of the right foot on top of the ball and immediately pull the ball back with the sole of the same foot. This move is used to fake a pass to a teammate.

When practicing footwork, you should attempt these different moves individually. Later, you must be able to combine them randomly. The faster your child can do it, the better control he will gain. Let me give you an example of a footwork combination:

1) Keep the ball in between your feet.
2) Do a push and pull.
3) With the sole of the foot, move the ball right and left.
4) Move backwards.

Dribbling 29

CHANGING DIRECTIONS

Place two markers 20 feet apart. Your child begins at one marker and dribbles the ball as fast as he can. He stops at the other marker by placing the sole of his foot on top of the ball. Then he rolls the ball backwards, turns around and dribbles back to the first marker. Young children should concentrate on accurately stopping at the marker. Beginning with second graders, shorten the distance between markers and focus on speed and accuracy.

Remember: Every time your child learns new footwork, he should combine it with the ones he already knows.

Extremely important: When the child dribbles, he has to maintain **peripheral vision**. He must be aware of what is happening around him. A simple way to teach this is to tell him to **look at the ball and quickly look up** while he dribbles. Repeat this process constantly. Beginning dribblers tend to keep their eyes solely on the ball and on the moves they are making with their feet while moving around the field. This causes them to lose their sense of direction and field position. More importantly, they are not aware of players running towards them or those already in front of them.

30   *Soccer in Your Backyard*

So far we have practiced some footwork for the children to develop body coordination, agility and ball control skills, which constitute the foundation of dribbling. These exercises are done individually and without opposition. Now we will add an opponent and proceed to practice how to attack and beat a defender. In order to do that, we need to learn fakes.

What is a fake? How do we perform a fake?

A fake is any deceptive move done with your feet and/or body to beat an opponent and either take or retain possession of the ball. When referring to fakes, I may also call them **soccer moves**.

There are many soccer moves you can use to beat your rival. The simplest is the oldest move in soccer history, the one that works best even today in professional soccer. This oldest soccer move is as follows:

1) While dribbling forward, pass your right foot over and to the right of the ball. Step and place your body weight on that foot. At the same time dip the right shoulder. This foot and body movement will deceive your opponent, who will move to his left side, thinking that you are going to your right.

2) Take the ball to the left side with the outside surface of your left foot, thus faking your opponent.

The faster you do it, the better it works. Try with the other foot if you feel more comfortable.

Dribbling

To beat an opponent with this fake in a real game situation, there are **TWO** important things you **MUST** do to be effective:

1) Change directions.
2) Change speeds.

With the ball under control, approach your opponent at a moderate speed. Then fake that you will move in one direction (as previously explained) but explode to the opposite side at full speed.

What is shielding?

Shielding is protecting the ball from your opponent.

When I teach shielding to children under the age of eight, I ask them to name their favorite desserts. The answers are always similar: chocolate cake and vanilla ice cream are among the most popular. "Well," I say, "what would you do if you had the dessert in your hands and someone came to take it away from you?"

"I won't let him; I will run away," is the usual response.

I continue by saying, "Let's pretend that the soccer ball is that delicious dessert. Place the ball between your feet. Now pretend that (I choose someone from the group) Michael comes from behind and tries to take it away, but the rule is that you can't run away. You can only remain in the same spot. How would you protect the dessert?"

The way to do it is to make a...

SANDWICH.

Then I ask the children. "What's your favorite sandwich?" They usually respond with "ham, cheese or peanut butter." "O.K. Let's pretend that you make a CHEESE SANDWICH in which you are the cheese, the ball is one piece of bread, and your opponent is the other piece of bread."

Dribbling 33

Therefore, the formula for good shielding is as follows:

S A N D W I C H
BALL - YOU - OPPONENT
BREAD - CHEESE -   BREAD

34   *Soccer in Your Backyard*

When you see an opponent coming towards you, but you can't run, your only option is to stay there and protect the ball. Follow these easy steps:

1) Immediately get in between the opponent and the ball.

2) Spread your legs **sideways** as much as possible. The opponent should be behind you, and you should stand sideways from him. Your shoulder should be facing him.

3) Lean toward the opponent. If possible, your elbow should be near his chest.

4) Move the ball with the foot which is furthest from the opponent. You will usually use the sole of the foot or the outside surface when shielding.

5) If the opponent moves to the right, you move to the right. If he moves to the left, you protect the left side.

6) Look around you. Find a teammate that is open, so you can pass the ball to him and move to an open space.

I encourage you to practice shielding with your child. It is very easy and extremely important for him to know how to protect the ball. Shielding goes hand in hand with dribbling and vice versa.

Every time we play a game in our backyard, it is usually the boys against the girls. When I am dribbling, my wife always tries to stretch the rules by grabbing me from behind, pulling my shirt or shorts and tripping me. I complain. The girls don't care. Everybody laughs, while the game continues. When we play at home, I really have to be good at shielding. It seems tougher now to play against my wife and children than when I used to play professional soccer!

36   *Soccer in Your Backyard*

Dribbling is an important skill to master. It builds self-esteem and confidence. It adds color to anyone's game. A child that dribbles not only shines "out of the bunch," but becomes a valuable asset for his team as well as a matter of concern for his opponents.

Let me tell you a short story about how dribbling helped to change a child's behavior and the relationship with his parents.

In one of my soccer camps, there was an eight-year-old boy named Alex. Physically and verbally aggressive towards others, he had a rebellious attitude towards his parents. The first day of camp, Alex would hit and bully other children, lacked concentration and didn't follow the coaches' instructions. By talking with Alex's parents, I was able to obtain more information about his personality and was glad to learn that he liked dribbling very much. The next day, I assigned a coach to work with him for a full day on dribbling. Every day we added one more child to join Alex's two hours of special training. We also focused on improving his discipline and respect. We taught him to channel his aggressiveness through soccer. Instead of hitting others purposely, he would use his skills to try to win; and that would be his satisfaction. Our challenges and his passion for dribbling made him focus on his strengths. Alex not only stopped hitting others but became more caring, friendlier and respectful. He attained second place in dribbling. His face regained a once lost smile. The entire second week, he greeted his parents every afternoon with a big hug, and I saw them leaving together, chatting and laughing.

DRIBBLING GAMES

RACES

As children love to race, I use races to teach them many concepts.

What do we learn by racing?

We learn **to carry or transport the ball**. This should be done by gently kicking the ball, keeping it as close as possible to the feet. In a race, most people tend to kick the ball forward and run. This is not the correct way to race with a ball.

When racing, we also learn **to change the speed** at which we run. This is done when you approach the target and move around it. Here, you need to slow down, then explode to reach full speed again. The change in speed is a key element for dribbling.

We also learn **to dribble in a straight line**. This task is difficult for small children due to their developing sense of direction and ball control. Races help them dribble in a straight line.

Finally, we learn **to be accurate in passing the ball**. In a relay race, you have to pass the ball to the teammate who is next in line. If you run really fast but don't make a good final pass, that mistake will cause your team to lose time. This would generate an advantage for the other team. Your team may lose due to such an inaccurate pass. Since it is difficult to pass accurately when you are going full speed, races are good practice.

SIMPLE RELAY RACES

Objective: To work on dribbling in a straight line, speed dribbling, turns, and ball control.

Players: Two to twenty (the entire team).

Materials: Two markers and one ball per team.

Rules: Place two markers 30-60 feet away from the starting point. Divide the number of players into two even teams. Each team member lines up single file facing the markers. The distance in between the two lines should be 12-15 feet. Each team has one ball which will be dribbled by the first player in line. At the coach's signal, the player, who is first in line for each team, begins racing by dribbling the ball to and around the marker and then back to the starting point. He then passes the ball to the second player in line.

Winner: The team which has all the players returns to the starting line first.

NOTE: When teams are uneven, the team that has one less player will have one member run twice. The first player in line will run and return to the end of the line. He will run again as the last player.

Dribbling 39

Variation: CHAIN RACE

Use the same set-up as for the simple race. The difference here is that the team members hold hands and make a strong chain. The first player in line has the ball and is in charge of dribbling it. This is a team race, and the rule is that the chain can't be broken. If a team is faster, but it breaks the chain, the team forfeits the race. You can play rematches and a final game.

This chain race is even more fun when there is a big group and each team has six or more people. I always mix parents and children in the same line. People tend to fall down in funny ways and break the chain. Everybody is bound to laugh and have a good time.

I always use these races for birthday parties or when friends come to visit. The photo below shows a group of kindergartners with their parents in Weston, Connecticut having a lot of fun.

SHARKS

Objective: The skills learned in this game are: Dribbling, ball possession and shielding.

Players: Four to twenty (the entire team).

Materials: Four markers and one ball per player.

Rules: Make a clearly marked square. The size will depend on the number and age of the children. The average size is 30 feet. Choose one player who will be the "shark" ready "to eat" the rest of the group. The shark stays outside the square, while the rest of the group, inside the square, begins dribbling the balls. When you yell "SHARK," the shark enters the square to try to kick the other players' balls outside of the square. Any player who loses his ball is out of the game.

NOTE: If a player's ball is kicked, but he reacts fast and stops the ball before it goes out of the square, he is still "alive" and can continue playing.

Winner: The last player who remains in the square in possession of his ball.

Variation: When the shark kicks someone's ball out of the square, that player also becomes a shark. Both sharks then make a chain by holding hands and going after other players. It is not valid if the sharks break the chain while kicking a player's ball out.

Dribbling   41

KING OR QUEEN OF THE MOUNTAIN

Objective: To practice dribbling, ball possession and shielding.

Players: Four to twenty (the entire team).

Materials: Four markers and one ball per player.

Rules: All players are inside a square of about 30 feet or any clearly marked area. Each player has a ball. At the coach's signal, children start dribbling and try to kick other players' balls outside the square while protecting their own. When a player's ball is kicked out of the square, he is out of the game. The players have to be dribbling all the time. No player can be standing still in a corner.

Winner: The last player with possession of the ball.

NOTE: If you are playing with a large group (15-20 players), as soon as three or four players lose their balls, shout "FREEZE" and stop the game. Make the area smaller and keep on playing. Repeat this procedure every time a few players lose. Reducing the size of the square shortens the time spent on the game to prevent the children who are already out from becoming bored and losing motivation.

U F O INVASION

Objective: To practice dribbling, teamwork and racing against the clock.

Players: Four to twenty. Players should be divided into four equal groups.

Materials: Four markers and at least one ball per player. To have more balls than the number of players is preferable.

Rules: The game consists of four groups of UFOs from different planets (children can choose names of planets) coming in their space ships to invade the Earth. Who will win the space war?

Place each group in a corner of a square (30-40 feet). Pile up all the balls in the center. Give players a number; i.e.,1,2,3. At your signal, player # 1 from each group runs to the center and dribbles one ball to his corner. One at a time, players continue coming to the center until all balls are gone. At this point, all the players scatter and "steal" the other team's balls. Players should continue dribbling as many balls (one at a time) as possible to their corners. They cannot protect the balls in their corners or tackle anyone. They only compete against the time that you set; i.e., two to four minutes.

Winners: The team who has the most balls in its corner when time is called.

3

PASSING

Professionals usually use the inside of the foot for passing, especially for short distances.

Why do most beginners kick with their toes?

The answer is simple: it comes naturally. If you didn't know anything about soccer, and I asked you to walk to the ball and kick it, you would kick it with your toe. Why? The toe would be the first logical point of impact with any object in front of it.

Why should we mainly use the INSIDE of the foot for passing?

We should use the inside, because it is the widest surface of the foot which, therefore, gives us more accuracy.

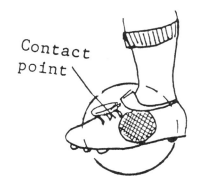

NOTE: Advanced players of any age may use not only the inside surface of the foot for passing but the outside, the top, the heel, the sole, or the toe as well. However, for teaching purposes, I emphasize the mastery of passing with the inside surface first. Then, when the player has successfully passed this stage, I recommend learning to pass using other surfaces of the foot and other techniques.

A WORD ON RECEIVING THE BALL

What is receiving the ball?

When someone passes the ball to you, the skill of collecting or stopping the ball is called ball control, receiving or trapping. When the ball comes on the ground (a low ball), the simplest way to receive it is by placing one foot sideways in front of the ball, stopping it.

For low and high balls, there are other techniques to control the ball, such as the instep, the thigh, and the chest which will be discussed in further detail in Chapter 5.

BASICS FOR PASSING

Passing is one of the most important skills in soccer. Through passing, you communicate with your teammates during a game. Equally important, passing constitutes the foundation for shooting. Good passing and shooting skills lead to goal scoring and winning games!

Passing

To effectively pass the ball:

1) Place the ball anywhere on the field.
2) Move a few steps backwards. (You need to have space between you and the ball.)
3) If you are right-footed, move a few steps to the left to approach the ball from an angle. (Lefties do the opposite.)
4) Go to the ball and hit it with the inside of the foot (along the base of the toe).
5) Follow-through. After your foot hits the ball, your foot and leg continue the swinging motion.

NOTE:

a) When you move to the ball and are about to make contact with it, you should plant your non-kicking foot next to the ball (about six inches away) pointing toward where you are aiming.

b) Right before passing the ball, you have to flip your kicking foot outwards in order to hit the ball with the inside surface.

PASSING EXERCISES

There are two basic passing exercises which come naturally every time two players walk on a soccer field. These apply even for professional players.

1) Simply pass the ball to each other. Communicate. Facing one another at a distance of about 12-15 feet, one player passes the ball, and the other receives it, controls it and passes it back.

2) Repeat the same exercise with the variation that players pass the ball and move (9-12 feet away). The player who receives the ball has to control it and look up to see his partner's new position on the field to accurately pass the ball back.

These two exercises are an essential part of all training sessions. They are the simplest and most effective passing exercises. If you ever go see a World Cup final match, which features the best players in the world, you will notice that as soon as a team walks on the field, its players spontaneously get into groups of two or three and begin passing the ball to each other. This serves not only as a warm-up exercise, but also as a way to "talk" to each other, to give each other confidence and support.

So, every time you walk with your child onto a field with a soccer ball, remember that the first thing to do is to "communicate" with him (practice passing).

PASSING GAMES

THE TWO CHAIRS

Objective: To practice aiming and passing the ball.

Players: Two.

Materials: Two chairs and a soccer ball.

Rules: Position two patio chairs with their backs facing each other, as if to create a makeshift goal. The players stand on opposite sides of the goal at a distance of about 12-18 feet. Each player has up to three chances to score a goal using the inside of the foot. After a goal, it immediately becomes the other player's turn.

In the beginning, and according to your child's age and ability, space the chairs relatively far apart from each other (six feet). After a few shots, narrow the distance between the chairs, until ultimately they are so close together that the space is only wide enough for the ball to get through.

Winner: The one who scores 10 goals first.

In the photo on the next page, Peter Scher, an eight-year-old boy, scores a goal with little space left between the chairs. Great accuracy!

UNDER THE BRIDGE

Objective: To practice aiming and passing while moving.

Players: Two.

Materials: One ball.

Rules: Your child will play the game first, and you will be his assistant. Begin by jogging in any direction. Your child should follow at a close distance while dribbling the ball. Suddenly, stop jogging and spread your legs **sideways**, making "a bridge."

Your child must hit the ball with the inside of the foot and try to score a goal between your legs. (See photo below).

Winner: If your child scores a goal, he earns one point; if he misses, he does not earn a point. Then you reverse roles. Whoever earns the first ten points is the winner.

Exercise progression: For small children between the ages of five and six, you should run very slowly in front of them, making it easy for them to score. Challenge older children by running faster, making ziz-zag moves, turning suddenly or making them shoot from far away. Also, you can make the children shoot at an angle, so they will be forced to curve the ball. This is not easy for children under the age of 10 to accomplish.

THE TABLE CHALLENGE

Objective: To practice passing under pressure.

Players: One. This is an individual challenge.

Materials: An old table or a plastic patio table and a soccer ball.

Rules: From a distance of about 10 feet, pass the ball against the table with the inside of the foot. As the ball bounces back, you have to continue passing it back while not allowing the ball to stop. You are not allowed to kick softly. It should be a regular pass. If the ball stops, you lose.

Winner: The one who can make the most passes in a row.

Try to use both feet. If the ball goes to the right, use the right foot; if it goes to the left, use the left foot. Remember to keep in mind the technique for good passing.

Sometime ago, we had a get-together at home with seven grown-ups and nine children. I invited them to take the table challenge. For this game, I used a patio table. As the referee, I did not play. We all had fun and played for more than an hour. The highest record of passes was nine. My children usually score at least 15 passes; but that day, in front of the crowd, they just couldn't do it.

Hint: You should always be "on your toes," or have what I call "quick feet" and be ready to react. Every time you kick the ball, you should quickly move backwards to get ready for the next ball, since you don't know if the rebound will give you a short or a long ball. Some people do the opposite by kicking the ball and moving forward, ending up in front of the table without a ball to kick.

Passing 51

CROQUET SOCCER

Objective: To practice aiming and powerful passing.

Players: Two.

Materials: Two balls. One per player.

Rules: Place the balls on the ground about three feet apart. Your child kicks his ball, using the inside of the foot and tries to hit your ball. If he hits it, he scores one point. Now it is your turn. Without changing the location of your ball, you must kick your ball and try to hit his. If you miss it, you do not earn a point.

Winner: Whoever earns 10 points first.

Passing 53

Variation: Challenge children who are skilled with a moving target. Begin by passing your ball to an open area. While the ball is still in motion, he should try to hit it with his ball. After he shoots, reverse roles.

THE BASKETBALL HOOP

Objective: To practice passing with the top of the foot (laces).

Players: One. This is an individual challenge.

Materials: A basketball hoop and a ball.

Rules: Stand in front of a basketball hoop. Gently throw the ball up. Let the ball bounce once; and when the ball is about to hit the ground for the second bounce, kick it from underneath with the top of the foot, trying to score in the hoop. Your body should be loose with your arms a bit open for balance. Do it over and over again and challenge yourself and your child until you get really good at it. Then challenge your friends when they come to visit.

Winner: Whoever scores 10 points first.

54   Soccer in Your Backyard

This is a very useful technique, not only for passing, but more importantly, for scoring goals. Apply this technique for scoring in a real game when you see that the goalkeeper has come out of the goal; in other words, he is several steps in front of the goal line. Kick a bouncing ball over the goalie and score.

Variation: If you don't have access to a basketball hoop, your child can still practice this technique in your backyard. With two markers make a goal. Stand at the goal as a goalkeeper. Then, step forward (about nine feet) from an imaginary goal line and have your child try to score over your head. In a real game, the goalkeeper will try to catch the ball by extending his arms as much as possible; thus, your child should kick the ball high enough to surpass your extended arms and hands.

Passing 55

Variation for advanced players: Ideally, you should have a few balls and the help of another person. Your child will perform the exercise, while you and a goalkeeper assist in the implementation of the exercise. The set-up is a straight line with the goalie standing at least nine feet in front of the goal line. The child should stand about 15 feet from the goalie. He should stand **with his back toward the goal.** You will have to be in front of him (4-5 feet) with all the balls. Gently throw the first ball over your child's head. Before the ball hits the ground, he should turn and kick the ball with the top of his foot over the goalie's head. This technique of kicking the ball with the laces before the ball touches the ground is called a **"volley."** The child should quickly turn to you for the consecutive balls. Small children should allow the ball to bounce once before they kick it. The pace of your serves should depend on your child's age and ability.

THE KITCHEN STOOL

This is another way to practice the laces passing and kicking technique. Your child sits on a high stool, bench or regular chair. Stand in front of him and gently throw the ball. As the ball comes to him, he has to kick it with the top of the foot so that the ball is hit into your hands. The kick should be firm.

This exercise is great for your child to learn how to control his kicking strength.

Passing 57

THE GARBAGE CAN

Objective: To practice aiming and passing with the laces.

Players: One to six.

Materials: A garbage can and a ball.

Rules: Place a large garbage can (like the one used for placing trash in a garage) on a hard, flat surface such as a driveway. The ball will bounce better on a hard surface, and this will help to give continuity to the game. The game consists of letting the ball bounce one time and kicking it into the garbage can with the top of the foot. Players should stand 9-12 feet from the garbage can.

Winner: The one who scores 10 points first.

If only one person plays, the can should be placed against a wall; so when he misses, the ball will bounce out either from the edge of the can or from the wall. It is great if one can score with one shot. However, if you miss, the idea is to continue shooting as the ball bounces off the wall or can.

It is more amusing when two or more players engage in this game. We usually place the big garbage can on the driveway, and all the players form a circle around it. One person lets the ball bounce and takes the first shot. If he misses it, and the ball goes over the can, whoever is on that side kicks it. The key is to keep the ball in continuous motion until someone scores.

GREAT IDEA FOR INTERMEDIATE AND ADVANCED PLAYERS!

SOCCER - SQUASH

To practice passing and shooting techniques, it would be ideal to go to a park which has a **squash court.** The court walls are great to improve passing and kicking, using all of the surfaces of the foot as well as the different ball spins, body positions, kicking angles and volleys. This is great training, especially for players who are older than 10 years of age. Why not try to play squash with your feet and head? Then your skills will work at a faster pace.

You don't need to know how to play squash. Just go to the squash court with your child (take a soccer ball with you) and make your own rules for your game! For example: The game consists in kicking the ball against the walls. The ball always has to hit the wall at least three feet above the ground. Only one bounce is allowed; and if the ball bounces twice when it's your turn to kick, your opponent gets a point. Whoever gets to 10 points first is the winner.

Once I was invited to play soccer on a squash court. My friend suggested we play with a tennis ball. After agreeing on the rules of the game, we started playing. It seemed like a long time before I could beat him. Regardless of the final score, the improvised game made me realize how much I needed to use all of my skills in order to compete.

Obviously, kicking a tennis ball is a lot more difficult than kicking a regular soccer ball. Nevertheless, it was a great experience; and we had a fun time.

Be creative. Improvise your own games to motivate your child to improve his skills. By involving your entire family in a fun activity, you will provide quality time together.

THE KEY ELEMENT FOR LEARNING IS

MOTIVATION.

4

KICKING

How do we kick the ball?

For a good kick, go through the following steps: Position the ball on the ground about 10 feet in front of you. If you are right-footed, move to the left side of the ball and approach the ball at an angle. If you are left-footed, move to the right side of the ball to obtain the proper **"kicking angle."** Finally, you should run to the ball and kick it.

IMPORTANT: When you are about to kick the ball, the non-kicking foot should be placed about six inches from the ball and pointed at the target.

What part of the foot should we use for kicking?

The answer will depend on what kind of shot we need. There are two types of shots: **powerful** and **technical.** Let's look at both.

For powerful shots, hit the ball with the top of the foot (laces). To accomplish this, the toes should be pointing down at the moment of contact with the ball.
For technical shots, like penalty kicks or free kicks, most players use the side surfaces of the foot with some spin.

After the foot hits the ball, and the ball moves forward, the foot has to **"follow-through."** The motion of shooting the ball does not finish at the point of impact. The same concept is found in tennis or golf. After a ball is hit, one should continue the swinging motion. Last but not least, the **upper body** is needed for a good kick.

When you kick the ball, your arms should simultaneously swing backwards. If a person is right-footed, the left arm should cross at the stomach level from left to right. The range of motion of the right arm goes from almost touching the right thigh to the middle of the back.

As the arms are swung, the whole upper body also swings, creating a **compression** which transports the upper body's power into the kick.

For powerful shots, you hit the ball with the middle of the laces. For technical shots, use the side of the foot (as shown in the drawing).

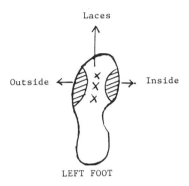

The same shooting technique applies when playing table pool: if one hits the ball in the center, it will go straight and low; if the ball is hit below the center, it will go high; and if the ball is hit on the side, it will spin to the opposite side.

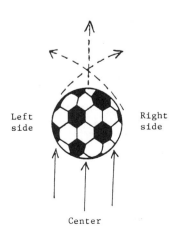

SHOOTING EXERCISES

TARGET SHOOTING

Children love shooting targets, and the good news is that almost anything can be used as a target. For example, a toy, a cone, a chair, a car tire or a mark on a wall can all be used; but **the most commonly used target is a T-shirt**. If you need a target, just bring an extra T-shirt, hang it anywhere and challenge your child to hit it. You can use the T-shirt as a target when playing in your backyard, in the park or on the soccer field.

As a child, I created my own ritual for shooting targets which I have used throughout my entire professional and coaching career. I always wanted to improve my shooting, and many times I convinced others to shoot with me or to be goalkeepers for me. However, most of the time, they would not do it for more than half an hour; and my intentions were to practice for hours. Few could withstand my long training hours.

I learned to motivate myself to achieve my goals. I would go in my backyard, take off my T-shirt, hang it somewhere and repeatedly shoot the target from different angles, low and high, using different spins. I have to admit that many times it was very boring; but I wanted to improve, and I knew that the only way to do so was through repetition.

I used a lot of self-talk for motivation: "Come on, Daniel, you can do it,...ugh, almost...next shot you can make it...left foot too, you've got to try it ...you have to be good with both feet... come on, 10 more minutes...a few more shots." I promised not to go into the house until I hit the most difficult target. I remember my mother would call me inside to eat dinner, to which I would always respond, "A few more shots, Mom, a few more shots." Even when I was playing professional soccer, when the coach finished the practice, I would stay for a couple of hours with teammates, or by myself, to shoot targets.

In my soccer camps and clinics, I challenge my assistant coaches to hit targets in front of the group of players. Shooting is like any other skill: if you don't use it, you lose it.

You could create your own ritual for shooting targets with your child. Shooting requires repetition, and the way to succeed could get boring. Encourage him to continue.

Kicking 65

TOUCH, TURN AND FIRE!

Objective: To practice shooting with the ball in motion in a game-related setting.

Materials: 3-5 balls to obtain continuity.

Players: Two.

Helpers: One. (If this exercise is used for team practice, the coach should assist in the game.)

    Position yourself at the goal. Your child should stand back about 15-20 feet (depending on his age) to shoot at goal. The child should stand with his back toward the goal, facing the helper who will have a few balls with him. The helper will extend one hand and arm forward. The child will run to the helper, touch his hand and then spread his legs. The helper will pass the ball in between the shooter's legs, who will turn and shoot as soon as possible.

    After the first shot, the shooter will run back to the helper. Repeat the routine as many times as balls are available.

IMPORTANT:

1) The helper should pass the balls at different angles to enhance shooting practice.

2) When the shooter is about to hit the ball, he MUST glance at the goalie to decide where to shoot.

You can easily test the latter, if you are the goalkeeper for this shooting exercise.

Stand on one side of the goal before the child turns. If he shoots the ball to you, even though the net is fully open on the opposite side, it is probably because he did not look or go through the thinking process in his mind. As his coach, you should emphasize the following: he should glance at the goalie and choose the best side to shoot. Many children make this costly mistake during games; consequently, they miss the opportunity to score easy goals.

Kicking 67

SHOOTING GAMES

FIRING ON THE GOALIE !

Objective: To practice shooting with the ball in motion.

Players: Two.

Materials: Two objects and 2-3 balls (to give the game continuity).

Winner: The one who scores the most goals from the first 10 rolled balls.

Rules: Create a makeshift goal, using two objects. Act as goalie, as you prepare to be challenged by your child's "soccer expertise." Children love to win against their parents when playing soccer games. If your child is between the ages of five and seven, I suggest you let him win most of the time. In time, challenge him more and more.

You are at the goal with a ball in your hands. Your child is in front of you at about 12 feet waiting to shoot. When both of you are ready, roll the ball to him (not too hard). As the ball approaches, he has to kick it without stopping it. Try to make it as fun as possible. Increase the speed. If he falls down, roll the next ball right away or dive to the side and spectacularly catch the ball. After a while, reverse roles. Take turns being "the champion." Reign as champion for a week; then allow your child to win, so he will be the champion the following week.

Make it fun! Enjoy it. If you do, I am sure your child will, too.

This exercise is the best and most simple way to improve shooting with the ball in motion.

IMPORTANT: The child should always shoot and move backwards to his original position to get ready to kick the upcoming balls.

Kicking 69

THE CAR TIRE

A car tire is ideal for shooting training. Its hole in the middle makes it very attractive for children. You can create many games with it.

GAME 1

Objective: To practice kicking at a low target.

Players: Two.

Materials: A car tire, two patio chairs, a ball.

Winner: The first who scores five goals.

Rules: Use two objects to support the tire in an upright position. At home, I always use two chairs (see photo on page 70). Both players stand at opposite sides of the tire. Your child will shoot the ball from a distance of about 12-15 feet (adjust distance according to his age) and try to make it through the hole. If he succeeds, he earns a point. Each player has three chances to score a point. If unsuccessful, the ball goes to the other player. When the entire family or a group of friends participates, it is great fun. This is also a great game for birthday parties! The photo on page 70 shows our family and friends playing this game. It was fun to see the children daring to beat the adults.

Idea: For children seven-years-old or under, place your head in the hole and dare your child to hit you.

70   *Soccer in Your Backyard*

NOTE: Once your child has "mastered" shooting from 12-15 feet, move the ball backwards and challenge him from a longer distance.

GAME 2
   Hanging a tire from a tree or swing.

Objective: To practice kicking at a high target.

Players: Two.

Materials: A car tire, a rope, 2-5 soccer balls.

Winner: The one who scores five goals first.

Rules: Hang a car tire from a swing or tree. This should be a fixed tire (tie it from the sides so the tire will not move). Make sure that the bottom of the tire is no more than three feet from the ground. Depending on the child's age, set the shooting distance. I suggest nine feet and up. Place all the balls in a line one next to the other. I call this the "firing line." The game consists of having the child attempt to kick the ball through the tire. If a ball hits the tire, the player scores one point. If the child kicks a ball through the tire, he earns two points.

NOTE: When you need to kick high, strike the ball underneath while leaning your upper body backwards as much as you can. (See Hint on next page.)

72   *Soccer in Your Backyard*

Idea: To make it fun for children seven-years-old or younger, stand behind the tire and put your head or buttocks in the hole. Dare your child to hit you. If he does, scream loudly and pretend it hurts.

High Kicking Hint: Your child will probably never play on a perfectly even soccer field. However, bumpy fields are good news for the beginning kicker. When the referee calls a fault, there is not a specific spot to position the ball for the kick. You can always move the ball around a few inches, even in the penalty kick spot. The trick is to put the ball on a bump. That way, the ball will already be higher than the ground level; thus, the kicker will be able to hit the ball underneath and kick the ball to a higher altitude. Don't forget to lean your upper body backwards as you perform the motion.

Variation for advanced players:

Moving Target: When you see that the child is improving at shooting the ball through the stationary tire, it is time to increase the game's difficulty. When he is ready to kick, swing the rope to create a moving target. With practice, your child should be better able to calculate the distance and the time that is needed to hit the ball through the moving target. For better results, use several soccer balls or volleyballs. Place one ball next to the other, creating a "firing line." As the tire swings back and forth, he should attempt to fire one ball after the other through the moving target.

SOCCER BALL FISHING

My eight-year-old, Michael, likes to go fishing. One day, I found a small, old net in the garage. As soon as I saw it, I invented a game for shooting. When Michael is not motivated to shoot at the T-shirt or the car tire, I ask, "How about going fishing?" He knows that I mean soccer ball fishing.

Objective: To practice kicking at different angles.

Players: Two.

Materials: One ball and a fishing net (Ideally 2-4 balls to give continuity to the game.)

Winner: The one who scores more goals after three sets of attempts. (One set equals the number of balls that you have available.)

Rules: Stand in front of your child at a distance of about 9-15 feet and hold the net to one side as a target. Your child will line up the balls one next to the other. After he shoots the first ball, quickly switch the net to the other side or lift it up in the air, so he has to adjust his aim to the new target position. Again, depending on the age of the child, make this easier or more difficult for him. For five- to seven-year-olds, make it very easy by placing the net low, eventually changing from right to left to make it more difficult. You can encourage beginners by moving the net to "catch the fish." Even if the kick is totally off, you should make an effort to catch it.

For eight- and nine-year-olds, try to place the net a little higher and still make the effort to get the balls into the net. However, when the child is more skilled, do not move the net to catch the ball.

Variation for advanced players:

If your child is skilled enough, hold the pole on your shoulder, so the net is behind your head. Challenge him to **CHIP** the ball (see next page) over your head and into the net. He can also kick the ball with the laces after one bounce. This would be challenging even for professional players. Children who think they are really good players could be hooked at attempting this particular feat for hours. It is difficult but rewarding.

Kicking 75

TO CHIP THE BALL:

The top of the kicking foot (exactly where the toes end) hits the ball underneath. As your foot makes contact with the ball, bend your toes upward and scoop the ball up, causing a backspin on the ball. **Don't follow-through.**

The non-kicking foot is positioned next to the ball as in a regular kick. The chip is very difficult for beginners and intermediate players. It takes lots of practice to attain the backspin and the height.

THE WOODEN RABBIT

We have a five-foot tall wooden rabbit that we love to use as a shooting target, because it is bright, colorful and very tall--a very attractive target for the children. I use my imagination to create different outfits for the rabbit. Sometimes, I hang a few carrots from his hands, giving us another target. We always change our system for scoring points. For instance, sometimes we decide to do the following:

If a player hits the rabbit's head, he earns 10 points; if he hits its body, he earns five points, and if its arms are hit, the player earns three points. As I previously mentioned, we change the point system each time to give the children the opportunity to participate in the decision-making process. When we decide to dress the rabbit, they take a lot of pride in suggesting ideas and taking action.

If someone walks into our backyard when we are shooting at our rabbit, at first glance, it may not seem like much is happening: just two children and two adults shooting at a target. However, for us it is a lot more than that. Before playing, we went through the process of choosing our target. Then, we dressed the rabbit, selected the point scale, the distance from where to shoot, who would go first, second and so forth and whether or not this would be an individual or group competition.

Notice that even before beginning this simple game, my wife and I have worked at developing many aspects of our children's personalities, such as self-esteem, motivation, leadership, decision-making and action-taking. We believe positive reinforcement

Kicking 77

on a daily basis in these areas helps our children establish and define their personalities while polishing their social skills.

A game could be simple with a winner and a loser, or it could be a great experience of learning while playing and having fun. It will all depend on your approach and motivation.

When children are playing and enjoying themselves, it is the perfect time for parents, coaches and teachers to "camouflage" their positive messages in order to fulfill any special need a child may have. This will help children overcome problems and strengthen their character, essential elements to develop healthy, well-rounded individuals.

May our rabbit story open your imagination to create your own targets and games based on what your children may like or need. Children are different as are their needs. Make every game a learning experience and quality time for the entire family.

78   *Soccer in Your Backyard*

5

BALL CONTROL

What is trapping?

Every player needs to be able to control the ball. Various techniques as well as different parts of the body are used to acquire good ball control. In soccer, the term for ball control is also known as **trapping**. During a game, when the ball is passed, the receiver has to trap it and quickly set it up for passing, dribbling or shooting.

As previously mentioned, soccer fields are not in perfect condition. This becomes a tremendous disadvantage when it comes to ball control. That's why it is so important to practice trapping.

In professional soccer, we spend countless hours developing this technique, especially under opponents' pressure. We simulate game situations mostly for strikers and defenders, combining trapping with shooting, turning and passing. In a fraction of a second, a player must be able to trap, turn and shoot the ball.

What are the different ways to trap the ball?

If you position yourself on the field to receive a pass, only one thing is certain: **you never know what kind of ball you will be passed**. It could be high or low, with or without a bounce or spin. For that reason, there are several ways to trap the ball.

We should picture trapping like receiving a **fragile present** from a dear friend. At the time of delivery, we first notice a huge sign that reads: "HANDLE WITH CARE." Thus, this special and delicate present needs to be cushioned, not broken.

I will walk you through a few scenarios to introduce you to possible situations and provide the tools to develop this skill.

TRAPPING LOW BALLS

As I briefly mentioned in Chapter 3, the **best** way to control a low pass is by simply placing your best foot sideways in front of the ball. When contact with the ball is made, withdraw the foot slightly. This motion will cushion the impact and absorb the ball's pace.

CROCODILE TRAP (LOW BALLS)

Ask your child to imagine for a moment that the foot with which he will trap the ball is a crocodile's mouth. When the foot is flat on the ground, the mouth is closed; but when the sole is up...the beast is hungry for balls!

The receiving foot should point toward the coming ball. As the ball approaches, just lift the sole, leaving the heel on the ground. Once the ball is in the crocodile's mouth, the top jaw closes a bit, pressing down on the ball for total control.

SHIN LEVEL TRAPPING

If the ball comes to you at your shin level, just lift your foot, flip it outwards (to stop the ball with the inside surface) and proceed to receive the fragile present (see photo). When contact is made, withdraw the foot slightly.

HIGH BALLS: THE INSTEP "PILLOW"

For high or dropping balls, the instep of the foot is a good "pillow." From a standing position, simply loosen up and keep your eyes on the ball. Estimate the spot where the ball will make contact with the ground. Move to that spot. As the ball approaches the ground, lift your foot (about 10 inches). The top of the foot will receive the ball. The foot should not be stiff. Your arms need to be a bit open to obtain a good balance. The knee should be bent. The body weight should be placed on the non-working foot. As the ball makes contact with the instep, gently lower your foot to cushion the impact.

The most common mistakes with this technique are as follows:

1) The body is too rigid, and the foot is totally stiff. Therefore, the ball bounces away.

2) The player miscalculates the spot where the ball will bounce; thus, he is too far away from the ball and is forced to fully extend the leg. The ball usually hits the shin and bounces off.

THE THIGH "PLATFORM"

The thigh provides a good platform for the ball to land. It is the widest surface available to control high balls.

To proceed, lift your thigh so that it is completely parallel to the ground. As usual, the arms should be a bit open for balance, and the upper body should lean slightly backwards. The contact point should be the mid-thigh. As the ball hits your thigh, gently lower it to absorb the ball's force. The ball will then drop to the ground.

For beginners, the difficulty is accurately trapping the ball with the mid-thigh. Often, the ball hits the knee and bounces off.

NOTE:

When trapping high balls, it is very important to move to the ball to accurately estimate the spot where the ball will make contact with the ground.

THE CHEST TRAP

The chest is another good platform for controlling high balls. For this trapping technique, the same general concept of cushioning the ball should be applied.

With your eyes on the ball, calculate the spot where the ball will land. Position yourself in that specific spot under the ball, so it will accurately make contact with your chest. Sharply arch the upper body backwards to create a good platform. The arms should be open for balance. Spread your legs apart and bend both knees. Next, apply the concept learned with the other techniques. When the ball hits the chest, slightly move the upper body backwards and further bend your knees to cushion the impact.

As the ball drops, you can make a second trap with the thigh or the instep before the ball reaches the ground. Usually, after controlling the ball with the chest, we combine it with the instep to bring the ball to the ground.

The parts of the body used to control the ball depend on individual preferences and game circumstances. Children should practice all the techniques.

Ball control is an extremely important technique which every player must perform well. Everyday the game of soccer is played at a higher speed and with more physical pressure. Thus, committed players should master the skills that will allow them to control the ball in limited spaces. Practice!

86   *Soccer in Your Backyard*

TRAPPING EXERCISES

FOR BEGINNERS

1) Lone Ranger

Start by standing in a stationary position. Throw the ball up in the air and trap it with the instep. Then, throw the ball up and trap it with the thigh. Finally, use the chest. Repeat the set. This is the best way to get a good feeling for ball control. At first, the ball should not be thrown too high.

Do you remember the FRAGILE PRESENT? Be gentle when throwing and receiving the ball.

Variation: With the ball in your hands, move around and throw the ball up and away from you (not too high). Follow the ball and trap it with any part of the body. In this way, it becomes more like a game situation.

2) Two players

a) **Low ball trapping**
Two players face one another at about 12-20 feet. The helper repeatedly passes a low ball with the inside of the foot. The receiver should alternate trapping the ball with the inside and the sole of the foot.

88   *Soccer in Your Backyard*

b) **Shin and knee-level trapping**

Using both hands, the helper gently throws the ball. The receiver lifts his foot and traps the ball with the inside. When the ball drops, he passes it back to the helper using the inside of his foot.

c) **Thigh trapping**

The concept is the same, but this time the helper throws the ball a little higher. The receiver traps the ball with the thigh, lets it fall directly to the ground and passes it back to the helper.

d) **Chest trapping**

Use the same concept. After trapping, the receiver lets the ball drop to the ground and passes it back to the helper. The player can trap the ball again with the thigh or instep before the ball touches the ground.

FOR INTERMEDIATE AND ADVANCED PLAYERS

This exercise is for two players. Use two objects to make a goal. The receiver will be the goalkeeper whose job is to stop the ball using any part of his body but his hands. The helper throws the ball (not too hard) to the sides at different heights and speeds. The receiver has to move toward the ball and trap it, using the techniques previously learned. After trapping the ball, the receiver passes it back to the helper. The helper can use his hands and alternate with some kicking. Count how many traps the receiver can make in 60 seconds. Then reverse roles.

Ball Control   89

ADVANCED TRAPPING EXERCISES

1) Thigh trap

Two players face each other at a distance of approximately nine feet. The helper serves the ball to the other player's thigh. The receiver traps it with the thigh; and when the ball drops to the shin level, he gently volleys it back to the helper's hands. Immediately, the receiver begins jogging backwards and waits for the second throw. Once the helper receives the ball, he begins jogging forward while he serves the second ball.

This exercise must have continuity. Once the ball first departs from the helper's hands, both players should start jogging slowly, one forward and the other backwards.

Variation: Perform the same exercise but trap the ball with the chest.

You can also use this exercise for practicing the following:

a) Heading
Instead of trapping the ball and passing it, the player, while moving backwards, heads the ball back to the helper's hands.

b) Instep kick
Use the same exercise format. As the ball comes, the player volleys it back to the helper's hands.

2) Trapping under pressure

This exercise is also for two players. Face each other at a distance of about 18 feet. The helper serves the ball and "attacks" the receiver as if he were an opponent trying to take the ball away. The helper waits until the receiver touches the ball before approaching. The receiver traps the ball, despite the opponent's pressure. He can either turn and keep possession of the ball for 10 seconds, or he can charge the opponent and try to pass him.

NOTE:

Generally speaking, children don't like to work on skills. Why? Simply because skills are enhanced through repetition, and that, after a short period of time, becomes boring for a child.

A good strategy for getting children to work on a skill is to present it as a challenge. A parent could say: "Let's go to the backyard to work on kicking." A better approach would be: "I bet I can beat you at shooting targets today. If you win, I'll buy you some ice cream, if you lose...."

Whenever your child gets bored or tired during play, take a break. Find a good place to sit and allow for meaningful conversation. This is an excellent opportunity to tactfully find out about school, friends and personal issues. This is the perfect time to use the soccer atmosphere as a stage for an anecdote about a similar situation you faced when you were his age or an imaginary story with some colorful character from whom your child may learn something positive to reinforce any immediate need he may have.

6

JUGGLING

Why do we need to juggle in soccer?

Besides being fun, juggling helps us develop ball control and acquire confidence and self-esteem. As I previously mentioned, I learned to juggle not with a soccer ball but with flowers.

I vividly remember my childhood days in which I'd juggle flowers for hours without end. During the summers in my hometown, I would passionately compete with the other neighborhood children to see who could beat the juggling record. Even today, I believe that this is the best method to learn how to juggle.

I encourage you to try to juggle a flower with your family. Not only is it different, but it will also provide a great challenge and entertainment.

Let's begin!

JUGGLING EXERCISES

How do we juggle with a flower?

You will juggle the flower only with your best foot. Pretend that you have a soccer ball in front of you. Now pretend you place your foot on top of the ball, causing your knee to bend. Open your arms a bit for balance. You are ready to juggle with your foot.

You can start with the flower on top of the foot. Begin kicking the flower into the air and keep juggling it as many times as you can.

HINT: Kick the flower a few inches into the air. Your non-kicking foot acts not only as your support, but more importantly, it is your only means of mobility. When you kick the flower, it will go a bit forward or to the sides. The key is to **follow the flower**. You do this by moving toward the flower, propelled by your non-kicking foot. **Never change your initial juggling position.**

Sometime ago, I challenged a group of friends who visited us to juggle a flower. The record was seven for the grown ups and six for the children.

JUGGLING ORANGES

This is also great fun. First try to juggle with only one foot. The technique is the same as with the flower. After you can successfully juggle five to seven consecutive times with your best foot, try to incorporate the other foot as well as your thighs and head. Good luck!

JUGGLING WITH A SOCCER BALL

FOOT JUGGLING

Use a soft soccer ball. The size of the ball will vary according to the age of the child. I recommend using a volleyball, as it is lighter than any regular soccer ball and allows for better control.

Use the same foot-juggling position and technique as with the flower exercise. Juggle only with your best foot and follow the ball wherever it goes, trying to make as many touches as you can. Keep the ball very low.

As a rule, the ball should never go higher than your knee.

THIGH JUGGLING

After you or your child can juggle the ball a few times with one foot, try to use your thigh. Begin by doing it in an ISOLATED way. Hold the ball out in front of you. Let it drop, and with the mid-thigh hit it back up to your hands. Then try it with the other leg. Hit the ball once and then catch it. Repeat this several times.

After doing this a few times, attempt to use the right thigh and the left thigh before catching the ball. The upper body should be leaning a bit backwards. The thigh surface should be horizontal each time it hits the ball. Little by little, increase the number of touches. It is easier to juggle with the thigh, simply because it is a wider surface.

**IMPORTANT:
Follow the ball!**

HEAD JUGGLING

Finally, attempt to juggle using your head. Spread your legs and place one foot pointing forward and the other foot three or four feet behind it, pointing sideways. This position will give you good support. Open your arms for balance. Throw the ball up and quickly reposition yourself directly under the ball. Hit the ball softly with your forehead. Every time you hit the ball, it should not go more than a few inches above your forehead.

IMPORTANT: Follow the ball, but always keep your legs spread apart and your feet in the same configuration.

96   *Soccer in Your Backyard*

After juggling with your feet, thighs and head and achieving at least a few consecutive touches with each of them, try to juggle combining all of them. For example, begin with the thigh and do three touches. Then, let the ball fall to the foot and do two touches. Finally, kick the ball to the head. I recommend starting with the surface with which you feel most comfortable.

The above-mentioned exercises are your building blocks for juggling. However, there are many ways to make your juggling more colorful and challenging. The only rule for juggling is that the ball must not touch your hands or the ground. So use your imagination to come up with different ways to keep the ball in the air. For instance, you could balance the ball on top of your foot for a few seconds. You might try to balance the ball on top of your head without bouncing it. Also, try sitting on the ground and juggling with your feet. After a few seconds, stand up and keep juggling. You could also hit the ball with other surfaces, such as the outside of the foot, heel, shoulders or chest. You could balance the ball on the back of your neck and get down to a push-up position to do some push-ups.

To get to this final level, it would take you or your child many years of practice. However, my objective is to help you understand the many possible ways to juggle in soccer.

RECOMMENDATIONS

Pay close attention to the position of your body beginning with the **foundations:** your feet and legs. **Balance** is a key element; keep your arms open.

The ball will move everywhere: forward, backwards, sideways. Follow the ball.

Most importantly, you should keep the ball as close to your body as possible. Don't hit the ball too hard, or it will be tossed too far away.

Try juggling. I promise it will challenge you and your family, providing hours of entertainment and fun. Motivate your child to try it. Watch him perform and correct him, so he understands the concept.

HEAD JUGGLING GAME

Objective: To head the ball back and forth between two players.

Materials: One ball.

Winner: Both players work together to set and then break their own records.

Rules: Two players stand facing one another at a distance of about 9-12 feet. The players pass the ball back and forth to each other, using their foreheads to keep the ball in the air as long as possible. They should count how many times they can pass the ball and establish a record. The players should try to beat their record over time. My wife and I have a record of seven.

98   *Soccer in Your Backyard*

THE ULTIMATE JUGGLING CHALLENGE IS...

TO JUGGLE A TENNIS BALL !

This is extremely difficult. However, you can surprise many people with a little bit of practice. Remember the flower? I hope so. Well, follow the same concept by using your best foot. The ball should never go higher than halfway between your foot and your knee. Also, try it with your thigh and head.

**Give it a try... just for FUN!
You'll be surprised!**

7

HEADING

Heading is one of my favorite techniques. My position in soccer has always been center-forward, and I have scored many decisive goals using the heading technique. I developed a good instinct for timing combined with the ability to jump high and perceive my opponents' mistakes.

If your child is going to play soccer, it is almost inevitable that he will have to head the ball sooner or later, especially if he plays defense or forward.

Why do some small children tend to develop a fear of heading?

In their first attempts, they don't get the right timing; and when the ball is thrown to them, they hit the ball with some part of the face, usually, the nose rather than the forehead. Believe me, that hurts! Thus, they have a right to complain.

The job of the parent or coach is to teach them proper timing and the right way to head the ball.

Once they learn the technique, it doesn't hurt anymore. They'll even feel great if they are able to score a goal.

How do we properly head the ball from a standing position?

As with almost all techniques, you need to have good balance and a good foundation. Spread your legs apart, placing one foot in front of the other. Open your arms a bit. When the ball comes to you, your eyes should be open. Lean your upper body backwards and keep the neck stiff. Calculate the timing. Then nod your head towards the ball, hitting it with your forehead.

Follow-through. You can head the ball in any direction.

NOTICE:

IF YOU HIT THE BALL, IT WILL NOT HURT.

IF YOU LET THE BALL HIT YOU, IT MAY HURT.

HEADING EXERCISES

FOR BEGINNERS

For children under the age of nine, use a ball that is soft. If the ball is too hard, deflate the ball a bit. Most of the time, I use a volleyball at home. Children tend to close their eyes as the ball approaches them. This not only diminishes the chances of properly heading the ball with the forehead, but it completely decreases the possibility of good aim. It may also be painful, because the ball may hit any part of the head or face. If it hurts, the children will fear using the technique; and that is what we are trying to avoid.

1) Your child should hold the ball with both hands and position it in front of his face at the height of his forehead. He should move his head forward and hit the ball several times with his forehead to get a feel for it.

2) From a short distance (about 4 feet), serve the ball to the child. Using his forehead, he should head the ball back to your hands.

3) The child has the ball in his hands. He should gently throw the ball up about a foot above his head. When the ball comes down, he should head it forward towards you. Repeat the exercise, until the timing is right.

FOR INTERMEDIATE PLAYERS

Stand in front of your child. Use both hands to gently throw the ball to him. After the ball is thrown, quickly change your position, moving a few feet to the side or backwards. Your child has to head the ball to you, directing it to your new position. You can vary the difficulty according to your child's skill level.

Variation:

Instead of serving and moving, place a target on the side and ask the child to hit it. The target could be very low, forcing him to head low. It could be placed at different height levels and angles. You can also create some games with items you may have in the garage or basement. For instance, place a garbage can on the side. See how many balls he can head into the can. Each goal is worth two points. If the ball hits the edge, he earns a point. After attempting to successfully head five balls into the garbage can, reverse roles.

FOR ADVANCED PLAYERS

THE JUMP

Soccer is a very fast and unpredictable game. Many times the ball is kicked higher than our reach. Thus, we have no choice other than to jump and head the ball before our opponent does.

Have you seen how basketball players jump and hold themselves in the air for a few seconds before actually shooting? In soccer, we do the same. I categorize jumping as another technique which requires practice.

How high can you jump? How about your child?

The only place where heights can become equal is in the air. A player who is six-feet tall and a player who is five-feet tall could be the same height when in the air fighting for the ball. The taller player might be able to jump only one foot, but the shorter player might be capable of jumping two feet. Therefore, the ability of the shorter player compensates for his lack of height. I have seen this scenario many times. It seems that taller players don't show as much interest in improving their jumping abilities. On the other hand, shorter players, conscious of their physical disadvantage, work harder to develop the edge to compete in the air.

I have scored many goals by jumping and heading a ball over a goalkeeper who has had the advantages of jumping and using his hands.

THE JUMPING TECHNIQUE

Keep your eyes on the ball, calculating the time and place where it will land. Jump as high as you can, trying to meet the ball at its highest point. Once you jump off the ground, arch your back, open your arms, bend your knees, and much like a basketball player, freeze yourself in the air for a second. Then your upper body and neck, which should be stiff, come forward, so you can hit the ball with your forehead.

To accomplish maximum height when jumping, I run a few steps, bend my knees, obtain a good impulse with my arms and jump only on my left foot. Even though I am right footed, practice made me realize that for some reason my left foot gave me better height levels. Some people, however, prefer to obtain their impulse from both feet at the same time.

106   *Soccer in Your Backyard*

8

THE OLD MATTRESS

An old mattress can be used to practice many difficult soccer techniques which require players to be suspended in the air. The cushion of the mattress is essential, as it provides a soft landing and helps the child to lose the fear of falling or hurting himself.

The mattress helps us with:

Side-volley kicks

Bicycle kicks

Flying headings

Goalkeeping

KICKING EXERCISES

THE SIDE-VOLLEY

The side-volley is a side kick in the air. You can teach it to your child in the following manner. Have your child stand on the mattress facing you. You will serve the ball to him. If he is right footed, pretend there is a goal and a goalkeeper on his left-hand side. Ideally, you would have a helper to act as a goalkeeper. Gently throw the ball to your child. As the ball comes, he should open his arms for balance and landing. Knees should be bent. As the ball approaches him, he should jump and kick the ball in midair to the left side, using his right foot. For a proper landing, after the kick, his left hand should make first contact with the ground (the mattress), followed by his left leg and buttocks.

CAUTION: Make sure your child repeatedly practices the landing technique on the mattress before attempting to do it on the grass.

110   *Soccer in Your Backyard*

THE BICYCLE KICK

This is the most spectacular kick in soccer. If your child scores a goal from it, especially an important or decisive goal, I can assure you he will make you the proudest parent on the face of the Earth.

A bicycle kick is a backward kick over your head, while the ball is in the air. Usually, you will be facing away from the goal, surrounded by defenders, pressed by time and space. When you see the ball coming towards you in the air, jump and kick the ball backwards as it comes. Let's do it step by step.

FOR KINDERGARTNERS

The child should lie face up on the mattress with his legs bent. Stand in front of him and gently throw the ball. The ball should go right above his knees for him to be able to perform the kick. As the ball comes to him, he should lift his good foot and kick the ball backwards. Besides the kick itself, this technique teaches us to calculate time and space. In the beginning, if your child misses the kick, it is a sign that he needs to work on timing.

FOR CHILDREN AGES SEVEN TO EIGHT

The child should sit on the mattress with his legs bent and his arms a bit open but not touching the ground. As the ball comes to him, his upper body starts slowly moving backwards. He should lift the non-kicking foot with the leg fully extended and pretend to kick the ball, although he won't. Then, he should quickly lift his kicking foot and kick the ball backwards. The motion of the upper body going backwards should be like a rocking chair. The non-kicking foot provides momentum and a point of reference to help calculate where to hit the ball.

Exercise progression:

FOR CHILDREN AGES EIGHT AND UP

Perform this technique by standing (NO JUMPING). Everything works the same way. The only difference is that the child lets his body fall backwards and supports the fall with his hands.

FULL TECHNIQUE

The child stands on the front edge of the mattress. The imaginary or real goal is behind him. You are in front of him to serve the ball. As the ball comes in the air, he jumps and swings his non-kicking foot up, followed by the other foot which then kicks the ball.

After the ball is kicked, the problem is...

L A N D I N G !

114   *Soccer in Your Backyard*

This is why I use the mattress to get used to the landing and to avoid inflicting bodily pain.

Let's follow the motion of the arms. For right-footed players, the left arm follows the left foot in the initial lifting. That helps with the impulse. The right arm stays halfway up, until the right foot kicks the ball. Then both arms should be fully extended toward the ground. The opposite arms and legs are used by left-footed players. Hands are the first to make contact with the ground, followed by the buttocks and finally the back. The landing itself is a tricky technique.

CAUTION: Make sure your child practices repeatedly on the mattress to perfect the landing, before he attempts to do it on the grass.

A bicycle kick is a perfect example of a good player's mind work. In a real game, when the ball is still in the air, the player has to think ahead, study his surroundings, the timing, the space and make up his mind to do the bicycle a few seconds before the ball approaches him. **A good player should know what to do with the ball, before he gets it.** In soccer, the average player does the opposite. First, he receives the ball and later figures out what to do with it. By then, he will probably have a couple of opponents tackling him and causing him to lose the ball. Teach your child to **think ahead** when he **does not** have the ball. For example: Where am I positioned?; Am I bunching up?; If I were to receive the ball, I would shoot it as it comes.

FLYING HEADINGS

You are familiar with the push-up position, right? Pretend that you are standing, and someone asks you to fall straight into a push-up. That's similar to what players do in soccer many times when trying to score a goal.

When a teammate passes a thigh-level ball, five or six feet in front of you, dive forward, as if you were jumping into a SWIMMING POOL and head the ball into the net.

For training purposes, pretend that the old mattress is a swimming pool. You and your child stand facing each other on either end of the mattress (see photo on the next page). When you throw the ball, he dives forward, heads the ball to you with his forehead, and lands on the palms of both hands, as in a PUSH-UP position. I have scored many goals using this technique. It is something that takes many defenders by surprise, because they never expect it.

Variation:

Place a second helper on either lateral side of the mattress. Repeat the same procedure of throwing the ball to your child. Instead of heading the ball to you, the child will head it sideways to the other helper. If the helper is on the left side of the child, when the child dives and is about to head the ball, he should move his head a bit to the right (to obtain an impulse) and hit the ball with the left side of his head. It is very important to work on heading the ball not only with the forehead but with both sides of the head as well.

116   *Soccer in Your Backyard*

Daniel scoring for Uruguay in 1986 using this technique.

The Old Mattress   117

GOALKEEPING EXERCISES

CATCHING AND DIVING

Young players love to be goalkeepers. If your child enjoys being a goalkeeper, take the opportunity to practice diving and catching the ball in the backyard.

TO CATCH THE BALL

To stop a ball that comes **on the ground,** you have two options:

1) To get down on one knee.
2) To bend from the waist.

The first choice is preferable, because it is the safest option. When the ball approaches, kneel on one leg while bending the other leg with the foot turned outward. Position this foot outward to ensure that there is no space left between the knee on the ground and the foot. To catch the ball, place your hands in between your knee (which is on the ground) and your foot. The palms of your hands should be facing the ball. Immediately after you make contact with the ball, bring it to your chest and bend the upper body forward, creating a " shell " to protect the ball.

The second option is to stand in the way of the ball, keeping the legs straight and together. Lean forward with your fingers almost touching the ground. Your palms should be facing the ball. When you catch the ball, immediately bring it to your chest.

IMPORTANT: Inexperienced goalkeepers run the risk of placing their legs too far apart and letting the ball slide through them, especially when the shot is hard.

To catch the ball **at the chest level or higher**, open your hands and spread your fingers as far apart as possible with both thumbs almost touching each other. If you pay close attention to your hands in this catching position, you will notice that they are in the shape of a **"W."** For this reason, it is called the **"W"** grip. Your hands should be behind the ball.

When a shot to the **abdominal level** occurs, catch the ball with the hands first and then absorb the shot with the chest. Bend the upper body forward to surround the ball in conjunction with the arms.

DIVING

When the ball is kicked **to one side**, the goalkeeper should dive sideways with his arms fully extended and catch the ball with the "W" grip. If the ball is kicked too far to the right of the goalie, it is better for him to dive and fully extend only his right arm and hand (to give him the longest possible reach.) In this situation, not catching the ball would be appropriate. Instead, the goalkeeper should either stop the shot with one hand or block the shot by punching the ball away. The same concept applies when the ball is kicked very high and the goalie perceives that it's not safe to catch the ball. Again, the goalie should just punch the ball away.

LET'S PRACTICE ON THE OLD MATTRESS

Your child is on one side of the mattress. Throw the ball to the opposite side. He has to dive sideways to catch the ball and land with the ball in his hands (see photo on the next page). If he cannot catch the ball, he should punch it away. Throw the ball at different levels. Every time the child catches the ball, he should immediately bring it to his chest while bringing up his knees and bending his upper body forward to protect the ball and himself from any opponent who may be coming toward him at full speed.

122   *Soccer in Your Backyard*

NOTICE: Even though Michael catches the ball, it's technically incorrect. His hands should be behind the ball. The photo below shows the correct form.

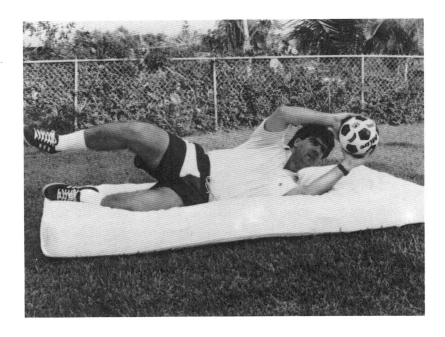

9

REACTION, AGILITY AND STRENGTH

Let's improve our fitness. Parents and children together!

In most sports, the players ought to be able to react quickly and run; they should be coordinated, agile, flexible and, in general, be in good physical condition. To accomplish this ideal level of fitness, parents should begin helping children at home at an early age.

I always incorporate the following exercises into races, games or personal challenges with my family and friends. I also make good use of them when I am teaching children.

REACTION AND AGILITY EXERCISES

GET UP AND RUN!

This exercise is especially good for children who are overweight, not too fast, or lacking agility.

The child sits down with his legs bent. Stand behind him with a ball in your hands. While he looks straight ahead and without any notice, throw the ball over his head. When he sees the ball, he has to react as quickly as possible. He should stand up and run to the ball. Before releasing the ball, you can tease the child by telling him to go! This simple exercise, with enough repetitions, should help a child react more quickly.

Reaction, Agility and Strength 125

Variation: Create the same scenario, but this time ask your child to close his eyes. He will react to the sound of the bouncing ball. **Quietly** throw the ball, and when it touches the ground, the child should open his eyes, stand and run.

MUMMY POSITION

Continue with the first exercise format and the same action-reaction concept. However, this time ask the child to lie down, facing up in a mummy position with his arms crossed, eyes open and muscles ready to react. Later, have the child attempt this exercise with his eyes closed and his legs bent.

PUSH-UP POSITION

Now ask the child to lie face down in a push-up position with his entire body touching the ground. Repeat the exercise.

126   *Soccer in Your Backyard*

MORE EXERCISES

1) The child sits with legs crossed, holding a ball in his hands. The exercise consists of throwing the ball up, then quickly standing and catching the ball before it bounces.

2) The child stands and holds a ball in his hands. He will throw the ball high and forward, then make a forward roll, stand and catch the ball.

Variation:
a) After the forward roll, instead of catching the ball, the child kicks (volleys) the ball into a goal in front of him or to a helper.

b) The player starts in an upright position with a ball at his feet. He makes a forward self-pass, followed by a forward roll and a shot in the goal.

COACHES: You can incorporate a goal and a goalie into all of these exercises. They are terrific combination exercises for improving agility and shooting skills at soccer practices.

STRENGTH-ABDOMINAL EXERCISES

The abdominal muscles are an essential source of strength and endurance for the body. The best exercise for strengthening the abdomen is **sit-ups.**

If your child is small, don't force him to do more sit-ups than he can do. Apply the natural process of exercise progression in which you begin with a low number of repetitions that increase with time. My intention is to provide you with some abdominal exercises using a soccer ball to make it more appealing to children. I want to instill in you the habit of exercising together with your family. In this fashion, adults stay fit and children have fun and realize the importance of exercise. For instance, every time an opportunity arises, my family and I play and exercise together. If exercising alone, my eight-year-old can do six sit-ups and my wife twelve. However, if we exercise together in a game format, having fun and cheering for each other, both can double their records. Exercising with others may improve your results.

ROWING TO SURVIVE

This particular exercise does not include a soccer ball, but my family and I enjoy it so much that my children begged me to include it in the book.

There should be four people seated in a circle with legs interlocked and knees bent for support. At the same time, they hold hands and pretend to be in a boat, lost at sea, with no food or water. To survive, they must make it to the nearest island which is 15 miles (15 sit-ups) away. They have no choice other than to row and row.

To be more effective and advance faster, the family has to row as a team. The strategy is as follows: parents go into the center (one sit-up), and children go out of the center (backward movement). Then, as the children sit up, the adults lean back. Both of these motions equal rowing one mile. Make sure the motion has continuity.

Begin with a low number of miles. Then every time you have an opportunity to do the exercise again, increase the miles. Row and cheer for each other. Hopefully, you will survive. Have fun!

NOTE: This sit-up exercise can also be done by two people.

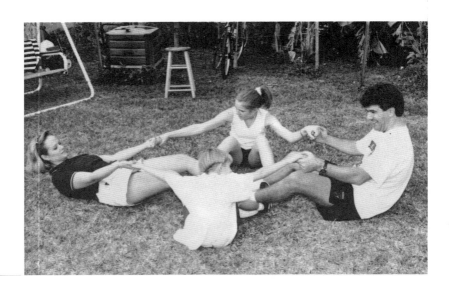

PAINFUL DELIVERY

One player and one helper are needed for this exercise. The one to exercise has to lie down, facing up. His legs are fully extended, and he has to hold a soccer ball in between his feet. The helper stands behind the player's head. The player who is on the ground has to grab the helper's ankles for support (see photo below). The exercise consists of delivering the ball from the player's feet to the helper's hands and back to the initial position as many times as possible. The helper should tap the ball every time it is raised up. After the initial delivery, the player's feet cannot touch the ground anymore. Ideally, on the way down, the feet should stop a few inches from the ground.

Variation: The previous exercise can be done without a ball. The only difference is that the helper grabs the feet each time and gently throws them back in any direction. The player has to avoid having his feet touch the ground. (This is my wife's favorite abdominal exercise.)

HEADING FOR SIT-UPS

Again, one player and one helper are needed for this exercise. The player has to lie down, facing up with his knees bent. The helper will stand in front of him holding a ball in his hands. The helper should softly serve the ball to the player who will do a sit-up. When in the upright position, the player will head the ball back to the helper's hands. Repeat as many times as possible.

Reaction, Agility and Strength 131

INDIAN BRIDGE

This exercise is for two people. They sit down facing each other with knees bent and legs interlocked for support. One has the ball. Both do sit-ups and exchange the ball each time they get to the upright position.

SOLITARY FIGHT

This is a one-person exercise. The person should lie down, facing up. His upper body should be lifted 30 degrees, supported by both elbows and forearms. Legs should be straight, and a soccer ball is held and pressed in between the feet. The ball should be lifted only four or five inches from the ground level, and the player should maintain that position as long as possible. When the ball touches the ground again, the player is disqualified.

This is an excellent but difficult exercise. Children love to challenge their parents to see how long an adult can survive. Establish your own record. See how many seconds or minutes you can "fight" the ball.

RUNNING

No doubt about it, running is one of the most important exercises to keep oneself in good physical condition. It enhances **ENDURANCE** and **RESISTANCE.** You can make running a family activity which will directly benefit the adults while exercising and entertaining the children, too. To instill in your child the habit of exercising at an early age is very important. Obviously, you should always measure the intensity according to the age of the child. For example, sometimes my wife and I decide to go for a half-hour run. Certainly, that would be too much for Michael who is only eight-years-old. However, since he wants to come with us, we agree that he either bikes or roller blades. If he chooses the latter, sometimes he gets tired, and we pull him along. As we run, he gets a free ride. He loves that part, and we think that he purposely gets tired; however, we are good sports and keep up the spirit.

The following exercise is for two teammates. They stand 10 feet apart, facing the same direction. One of them has a soccer ball. Both players start running slowly. The exercise consists of running and passing the ball back and forth to each other, like they would do in a regular soccer game. **The pass has to be diagonal and forward with the inside of the foot.** The player on the right has to use the right foot and the one on the left, the left foot. After reaching the landmark, they will turn; thus, each will then pass with the opposite foot. This is a simple but very effective exercise to practice running and passing in a game-related setting.

134 *Soccer in Your Backyard*

10

PROGRAMS TO BE CONSIDERED

EXCHANGE PROGRAMS AND INTERNATIONAL PROGRAMS

I strongly believe in the positive effects a sports exchange or international sports program can bring to our youngsters. A whole new world of different cultures, languages and customs suddenly opens, and much growth can occur. Values can be reshaped and solidified. Perspectives can be broadened.

As a member of a soccer team at nine-years-old, I began traveling outside my home town. I loved the exchange programs, because I got to stay with families from other cultures and backgrounds. They provided me with a wide spectrum of values and emotions which I compared with my own. I then assimilated some values and disregarded others.

Combining the above-mentioned experience with the soccer tournaments and the interaction with new friends my own age, each program was a great adventure of fun, enrichment, self-discovery and knowledge.

136   *Soccer in Your Backyard*

Each program brought me a step closer to molding a stronger and more mature personality. These trips were well-planned by our parents. They were established as part of a reward system for a good school trimester or year. The rule was that a good report card would guarantee a place on the traveling team. I vividly remember that the news of a new trip spread like wild fire, and we would try our very best in school. Teachers would even notice the difference in motivation.

The common denominator of these programs was FRIENDSHIP. On each trip, I met many new people but always truly connected with three or four. Even today, I am close friends with people I met in different parts of the world through soccer tournaments or exchange programs. Besides visiting one another and writing to each other, we have helped each other throughout the years on various occasions.

I feel that there is something magical about friendships that originate from a sports competition, a special bond which seems to grow stronger with time despite any distance.

Each day more and more parents are welcoming the idea of participating in these types of programs. They realize the positive benefits for their children and feel a sense of accomplishment by providing cultural awareness to the visiting children.

In order to continue my passion for these programs, I have been organizing and conducting these exchange programs for a number of years. In our last program, we brought a team of fourteen-year-old boys from Colegio Interamericano of Guatemala to Weston, Connecticut. Once the town knew about the event, many families immediately offered their homes to host our visitors.

The week-long program was a beautiful experience for our families, the Guatemalan children and their parents. They visited and played soccer in three different towns, and they learned about the American culture and school system. The Guatemalans delighted us with presentations on Guatemala, its people, culture and customs. They also visited New York City, the Statue of Liberty, the Twin Towers and Rockefeller Center. The visit coincided with the Fourth of July, and we celebrated with the traditional barbecue and fireworks.

On the last night of the program, my wife and I really opened our home to our new friends. The director of the Guatemalan team booked the returning flight from a New York airport at 6:00 a.m. The town of Weston, Connecticut is about an hour away from the airport. Instead of making all the hosts get up and drive in the middle of the night, we decided the entire team should sleep at our home! The farewell and the promise to visit them in their homeland marked the end of another life-changing experience.

The game of soccer has taken me to many different places around the world. It has made me interact with people of all races. It has given me moments of happiness and, also, some moments of disappointment. Above all, soccer has opened my eyes to the world, giving me the wonderful opportunity to grow and develop as a well-rounded individual.

SOCCER CAMPS

A week-long soccer camp is equivalent (skill-wise) to approximately one year of soccer training in a recreation or after-school program.

Camps are the ideal environment to improve skills. First, they are run by professional or former professional players who, themselves, have been in all levels of training and competition. Their vast experience and knowledge, which were mainly acquired in other countries, are advantages from which children can benefit. Also, the professionals who run the camp programs are, in general, very knowledgeable in working with groups of children. During the year, they run camps and clinics in different towns or in other countries and are exposed to a variety of working conditions. Because of this wealth of experience, they have developed well-balanced, week-long camp programs.

During a typical week of soccer camp, one main skill is taught per day. Children are divided into groups according to age and ability (beginner, intermediate and advanced levels). As the week progresses and children improve, they are moved to different skill levels.

Another advantage of a soccer camp is that it builds self-esteem and confidence. Camps usually have one hundred or more children from different towns. This makes for an exciting, challenging and rewarding experience for all children. After working individually and in small groups with players who lack confidence, a good coach will have the children demonstrate some skills in front of the entire camp. To perform in front of an audience of one-hundred peers is certainly a true measure of nerve, courage and confidence. My assistant coaches and I carefully prepare these skill demonstrations, especially for children who are shy and lack confidence. The round of applause and cheering they receive from the crowd becomes a priceless, emotional reward which definitely helps to break the shyness barriers inhibiting their personalities. Learning, fun, friendship and camaraderie are in general the common denominators of soccer camps.

SOCCER CLINICS

A soccer clinic is a soccer class taught by a professional soccer player or by an experienced coach. The clinic usually lasts from an hour to three hours, and in general it focuses on a specific skill or subject. Groups are small with parents usually present, making it ideal to exchange questions and answers between parents and coaches. I strongly recommend soccer clinics. First, they provide a great opportunity for parents to witness the skills being taught firsthand. Also, in a short period of time, questions regarding the game can be answered, and difficulties with certain skills can be overcome for the benefit of parents and children.

PARENT CLINICS

Parents learn the basic soccer concepts, skills, and do's and don'ts which prepare them to better help their children to have a good soccer experience. I highly recommend parent clinics.

11

PARENT-COACH RELATIONSHIP

A COACH WITH THE RIGHT APPROACH COULD BE A GREAT INFLUENCE IN YOUR CHILD'S OVERALL DEVELOPMENT.

MY APPROACH WITH PARENTS

There are many responsible coaches who are knowledgeable and child-oriented with integrity and good character. If one of those coaches happens to be your child's coach, you may have an excellent opportunity to get to know more about what is happening with your child. Furthermore, by means of the sport, the coach can help your child overcome most of his special needs, such as aggressiveness, low self-esteem, lack of leadership skills or shyness.

Good coaches with the intention to help parents are, or should be, a natural BRIDGE between parents and children. As previously mentioned, children don't always open up to parents when they are facing a difficult situation or problem; however, it may be more likely that they will talk to the coach.

Parent-Coach Relationship 141

If the coach is friendly and creates a good atmosphere of trust and fairness for his team, children will trust him and be confident enough to share their personal concerns, worries or fears, as well as their thoughts, dreams and aspirations.

As a parent, you should talk to your child's coach about your child as early as possible in the season. Make him aware of your child's strengths and weaknesses. It is important to inform the coach about any situation which may be temporarily affecting the child emotionally, such as a divorce or serious illness in the family. That information will help the coach make an accurate assessment of the child and prepare an initial plan of action to meet the team's requirements and the child's needs.

In our programs, my staff and I have established this method of open communication with parents. We have been able to help hundreds of children through soccer, not only by improving their soccer skills, but more importantly, by enhancing their personalities and social skills.

Every time a parent approaches us with a special concern about a child, we always agree to help, especially if the parent is willing to become "our assistant coach at home." Let me elaborate about the parent-coach relationship.

Let's create a scenario. Your son is shy to the point that it has become a matter of concern for both parents. If you share that concern with my staff and me, we will create many different situations in our training sessions to help him overcome his shyness. First, the coaches begin by playing a fun group game in which everyone introduces himself. Each player should memorize the rest of the players' names. We will ensure that all the children feel good about the

142   *Soccer in Your Backyard*

group. When the time comes to make teams for that practice, we name your child captain of one team. He will be able to pick his own teammates, and we will give instructions to the teams that both captains should report to the coaches and vice-versa. This way, the child will feel important, and, as captain, he will have to lead the group with the support of the coaches. During the game, we may even create situations for him to score a couple of goals.

In only one training session we have worked on boosting his self-esteem, motivation and leadership abilities. Can you imagine how many opportunities we would have during a soccer season or a full week of soccer camp to help your child overcome his shyness?

I want to emphasize that at the same time we are using the group to help your child overcome his shyness, the same exercises, games or scrimmages are helping the rest of the group. We do this while simultaneously teaching soccer skills and the understanding of the game.

For knowledgeable coaches, conducting a training session is like driving a car. The driver is able to simultaneously perform many different tasks, such as driving, listening to the radio and being aware of cars and traffic signs.

There is a magical chemistry between a coach and a player. Children look up to coaches as role models. Based on this fact, you have a golden opportunity to improve your child's overall development, if you channel your concerns through a coach.

Besides exploring the above-mentioned concept, your approach with your child's coach should always include the following objectives:

1) **Skills:** Your first concern is to make sure that your child improves his soccer skills. Witness your child's training sessions and games as much as possible. From the sideline, listen to the coach's instructions. Observe the drills. Try to understand the concepts behind the skills and techniques. Your questions to the coach should focus on the improvement of specific skills: How can my child improve his kicking, dribbling, etc.? Based on the coach's feedback and the games and exercises you already know, whenever possible challenge your child and reinforce his skills at home.

2) **Physical characteristics:** Look at your child from the physical point of view. Is he a slow runner; does he lack agility or coordination? Express your concerns to the coach and ask for his advice on how to improve what your child may be lacking. The coach can suggest some exercises to do at home. For example, there are often children who don't run correctly. They may run on their heels or plant the entire sole of their feet as they run. Also, it is common to see strong children who can't kick the ball hard enough when compared to other teammates. They don't know how to use their upper body's strength. Fortunately, soccer offers many different field positions which allow a good coach to find a "job description" for all children, regardless of their physical characteristics. For example, if the child is agile with some ability, he can play forward; if the child is overweight and slow, he can help the team in defense.

144   *Soccer in Your Backyard*

3) **Personality:** Observe how your child relates to the rest of the group. Compare it with your feedback from his teacher and his behavior at home. Share your point of view with the coach. You can suggest to the coach different things such as to group your child with one or two other players of similar characteristics or try to implement a strategy or some type of reward system. Remember the concept in the beginning of the chapter. Coaches can be very helpful with the above issue.

Often I have children going through a period when they become very aggressive, not only verbally but also physically. In those cases, my assistant coaches and I teach those children to channel their anger through soccer. Instead of hitting someone out of frustration, they train really hard, improve a specific skill and soon respond to a provoking child not physically but by technically "beating" him at a certain skill and feeling a sense of relief.

If your child is nine-years-old or younger, let me give you some examples of a few other positive results you can easily accomplish with the help of a coach. The coach can suggest the following tasks to a young child:

To go to bed at a certain time.
To do homework or school projects.
To read more.
To try to learn a parent's foreign language.
To team up with certain children.

The youngster may do them simply because the coach told him to do so. Amazingly, children will respond. Try it, and you may be surprised at the results.

12

IF YOU GET INVOLVED...

In many schools, teachers have overcrowded classes, tight schedules and demanding lesson plans. Taking this into consideration, parents sometimes volunteer in schools to establish good communication with teachers. This helps avoid misunderstandings and allows parents to react quickly to problems that may occur.

Soccer is like school, and coaching is like teaching.

Therefore, when you enroll your child in a soccer program, it is like placing him in a small school. You should have the same approach as with school to ensure that the child will have a positive and rewarding soccer experience.

146 *Soccer in Your Backyard*

Coaches are teachers; therefore, they face the same situations I mentioned previously. Besides, coaches usually have a second job or are involved in other activities, and managing these responsibilities can cause stress. A coach might unintentionally hurt your child's feelings. A joke, a gesture or a comment could be misunderstood and cause some emotional harm to your child. When something goes wrong, children don't usually talk about it immediately; and that makes it extremely difficult for parents to perceive that something is not right. When children arrive home from school or practice and we ask them, "How was soccer?," the answer is either "fine, o.k., great or cool." Eventually you notice things are not really fine with your child. Take the initiative to make the coach aware. During practice time, the coach may be able to create an opportunity for your child to express what is really affecting him.

Fortunately, coaches love children; and they are used to dealing with difficult situations which might occur in any group sport. Moreover, coaches are generally very receptive to parents and are willing to fully cooperate in working things out for the benefit of the child.

With this in mind, I suggest you allocate some time to your child's favorite sports and get involved as you would with his school. I would like you to consider two basic reasons for you to get involved in your child's soccer program.

1) You will be able to react quickly to any incident or misunderstanding that might occur. Being present will allow you to work it out with the coach almost immediately after an incident occurs.

2) Being involved means you can easily relate your personal experience and background to help your child's team and Soccer Club. Moreover, if your child sees that you are motivated about his team and are always around to help, the results may be as follows:

a) He will be more motivated to improve.
b) He will be proud to think that if soccer is important for him, it is important for you too.

I personally know of several parents in different towns who first got involved by going to practices or camps to oversee the coach-player relationship and make sure everything was fine with their children. They even stayed 15-20 minutes after practice to ask technical questions. Shortly after, they became assistant coaches for their children's teams; and within two years, they became presidents of the Soccer Clubs in their towns. Some of these parents now head soccer organizations and are able to institute healthy and necessary changes. Each program benefits approximately 500 to 1700 children and their families. I have personally witnessed the success of these presidents and their programs.

What a great difference those parents have made for so many children!

148   *Soccer in Your Backyard*

YOU CAN GET ACTIVELY INVOLVED IN SOCCER BY DOING ONE OF THE FOLLOWING:

- Assist the coach at practices or games.
- Become a coach.
- Organize team meetings, special events, parties.
- Transport players to games and/or practices.
- Provide refreshments.
- Promote public relations (i.e. newspaper articles).
- Provide First Aid.
- Provide or be in charge of equipment for the team.
- Become a team manager.
- Serve on the Soccer Board of Directors.

Another important aspect of being an active participant is that you are closer to coaches; thus, you have more opportunities to ask questions. If you attend practices, you will be able to see the skills taught firsthand. Therefore, you learn more about the sport and are realistically capable of helping your child to improve and understand the game.

Personally, I encourage parents to come to our programs as much as possible, especially at the beginning of the season when I run a soccer clinic for them. At the clinic, I explain my philosophy, my approach to coaching and the fundamentals of soccer. I also emphasize the most common mistakes young players make and show parents how to solve them.

As a coach, I encourage parents to learn the same techniques the children are taught. I try to teach both parents and children alike. That way parents can understand the concepts behind the drills.

If You Get Involved... 149

By learning more about soccer, you will be able to make the time spent together with your child more enjoyable.

Attend your child's practices and learn first-hand from his coaches. Participate in clinics for parents. Read. Watch videos. If you decide to actually coach a team, there are short courses which will teach you what you need to know. I encourage you to contact any board member of your local Soccer Club for further information on the subject.

Generally speaking, the role of the soccer parents is to transport their children to and from practices or games. Parents need to urgently change this "spectator approach" and become "part-time architects" to design their plans with a solid foundation, upon which they can build their children's soccer experiences. Soccer clubs and schools provide the best programs possible, while coaches teach and help to run them. Ultimately, parents should take center stage by playing the "protagonist" role to lead the story of their children's soccer years to a rewarding, positive life-learning experience.

Monitor your child's participation in sports closely. Make sure that your support fuels his motivation and development while you keep a close eye on the entire program. Ensure that your child receives all the benefits the sport can give him.

I encourage parents to actively participate in soccer. Learn as much as you can. Volunteer for your child's team and for your Soccer Club. Besides making a world of difference in your child's sport experience, your ideas and drive could help to continue shaping and improving the youth soccer movement.

CONCLUSION

If you have gained some more knowledge about soccer; if you have played and enjoyed at least one game presented in the book; if your creativity and imagination have been sparked; if your child has thanked you for playing one of my games with him, and you have noticed a smile of gratitude for your efforts; if you have considered getting more involved in soccer by helping your child's team or your town's Soccer Club; if you have improved communication with your child and with your child's coach; if you have spent more time in your backyard or at a park with your family, united through a soccer ball and enjoyed more quality time, I can happily say that it was certainly worth each and every one of the countless hours I have spent writing this book...with your family at heart.

Remember that motivation, persistence and patience are the key elements for overcoming all difficulties your child may encounter.

You, the adult, possess a wealth of positive life experiences which could easily be channeled to your child through the sport he loves. Play together. Make the sport a family activity. Team up. Create stories about sports. Invent characters. The more colorful and extravagant they are, the more the child will remember the stories and the positive messages behind them.

Children are like sponges, ready to absorb any information that may come from you. Communicate with love, motivation and consideration, since these are the best frequency channels into which your child's mind and heart will tune.

Conclusion   151

Look at the sport that your child loves as a vehicle that can take you to many places which otherwise may have seemed inaccessible. Let soccer be the means by which you reach and influence your child's values, feelings, personality, self-esteem and self-confidence.

GLOSSARY OF COMMON SOCCER TERMS

Bicycle kick: A backward kick over your head while the ball is in the air.

Center-Forward: Player positioned on the front line and whose main job is to score (also called the **striker**).

Centering: Passing the ball from a wide position on the field into the opponent's penalty area (also called **crossing**).

Charging: Legally pushing the opponent off balance, using shoulder-to-shoulder contact.

Chip: A high kick where the top of the foot hits the bottom of the ball. You then bend your toes upward, scooping the ball and causing a backspin.

Clearing: Kicking the ball outside of your own goal area in any direction, just to get the ball away.

Combination play: When two or more players through a series of short passes make an offensive play.

Corner kick: A free kick from the corner flag area by the offense after the ball has been kicked out of bounds (over the goal line) by an opponent.

Covering: Providing defensive support for a teammate.

Glossary of Common Soccer Terms 153

Dribbling: The ability to maneuver the ball with all the surfaces of your feet to maintain possession and control of the ball.

Fake: A deceptive move done with your feet and/or body to beat an opponent and either take or retain possession of the ball (also called **soccer move** or **feint**).

First-time: Passing or shooting the ball without first stopping it.

Follow-through: Allowing your foot and leg to continue the swinging motion after a kick or a pass.

Footwork: Foot coordination when dribbling.

Forwards: Players positioned on the front line, whose main role is to attack and score goals.

Foul: An infraction of the rules of the game.

Free kick: A dead-ball (stationary ball) kick awarded to your team after an opponent has committed an infraction.

Fullbacks (Backs): Players positioned closest to their goalie whose main role is to help defend their goal.

Goalkeeper: The last defender and the only player allowed to use his hands in the penalty area.

154   *Soccer in Your Backyard*

Heading: Shooting or passing the ball with the head.

Instep: The top of the foot (also called **laces**).

Kicking angle: The angle needed to approach the ball for a proper kick or pass. Right-footed players should stand to the left side of the ball before kicking. Left-footed players should stand to the right side of the ball.

Marking: Guarding an opponent.

Midfielders: Players positioned in the center of the field whose main role is to act as links between the defensive and offensive lines (also called **halfbacks**).

Non-kicking foot: The foot that is used for support and does not perform kicking, passing or dribbling (also called **stationary foot**).

Penalty kick: A direct free kick taken 12 yards from the goal line. When a player commits a major infraction in his own penalty area, the referee will award a penalty kick to the other team.

Save: When a goalkeeper stops a shot from an opponent either by catching or deflecting the ball.

Shielding: Protecting the ball from your opponent (also called **screening**).

Glossary of Common Soccer Terms **155**

Shooting: Kicking the ball toward the opponent's goal in an attempt to score.

Side-volley: A side kick in the air.

Sliding kick: When a player slides on the ground into the ball to perform a kick.

Sliding tackle: When a player slides on the ground into the ball in order to take the ball away from an opponent.

Tackling: Using the feet to take the ball from an opponent.

Throw-in: The way to restart the game after the ball has gone out of bounds by throwing the ball (with the hands) back onto the field.

Trapping: The skill of collecting or stopping a moving ball (also called **ball control** or **receiving**).

Volley: The technique of kicking the ball in midair with the top of the foot (laces).

"W" grip: The way goalkeepers catch the ball at the chest level or higher. They open their hands and spread their fingers with both thumbs almost touching each other in the shape of a "W."

Wall Pass: A pass to a teammate followed by a return to you on the other side of the opponent (also called **give-and-go**).

ATTENTION:

SOCCER ORGANIZATIONS, SCHOOLS, NON-PROFITS ORGANIZATIONS AND YOUTH GROUPS:

Discounts are available on bulk purchases of this book for fund raising and educational/training purposes. Special books, booklets or book excerpts can also be created to fit your specific needs.
For ordering, please write to:

**Reneda Publishing House
Soccer in Your Backyard
P.O. Box 170710
Hialeah, FL 33017-0710**

HOW TO CONTACT THE AUTHOR

Daniel dos Santos and his organization, Global Youth, provide different programs for selected schools, soccer clubs, soccer teams, towns, non-profit organizations nationwide and in several countries. The programs offered are: Soccer camps, after-school soccer, weekend clinics and international tournaments. Requests for information about these services and inquiries about availability for speeches and seminars should be directed to the following address:

**Global Youth Sports
201 Hurd Avenue
Bridgeport, CT 06604**

A NOTE FROM THE PUBLISHER:

If, after reading this book, your family invents a game which you all enjoy and play at home, or you have true stories of children who have improved any aspect of their personalities and behavior through any sport, we would like to hear from you. Please send us the name and description of the game(s), with a photo of your family members playing it at home and/or the stories. They could be included in our next book!

PLEASE SIGN AND FILL THE RELEASE FORM BELOW WHEN SENDING GAMES, PHOTOGRAPHS OR STORIES.

I hereby authorize Daniel dos Santos to use the game(s), photograph(s) and/or stories of my family and I or in which I may be included with other participants, in any medium and for any purposes whatsoever, including without limitation, all promotional and advertising uses, and other trade purposes as well as using my name in connection therewith if Daniel dos Santos so desires; and the right to copyright said game(s), photograph(s) and/or stories in his name.

I hereby release and discharge Daniel dos Santos from any and all claims, actions and demands arising out of or in connection with the use of said game(s), photograph(s), and/or stories including, without limitation, any and all claims for invasion of privacy and libel.

I represent that I am over the age of 21 and that I understand the contents hereof.

SIGNATURE_____DATE_____

Please Print
NAME_____

ADDRESS_____

CITY_____STATE_____ZIP_____

PHONE: (_____)_____

Please, mail to: Reneda Publishing House
                     P.O. Box 170710
                     Hialeah, FL 33017-0710